Maine Coon Cats

Maine Coon Cat Owner's Manual

Maine Coon Cat care, personality, grooming, health, training, costs and feeding all included.

By

Elliott Lang

ALL RIGHTS RESERVED. This book contains material protected under International and Federal Copyright Laws and Treaties.

Any unauthorized reprint or use of this material is strictly prohibited. No part of this book may be reproduced or transmitted in any form or by any means, electronic, mechanical or otherwise, including photocopying or recording, or by any information storage and retrieval system without express written permission from the author.

Copyrighted © 2014

Author: Elliott Lang

Published by: IMB Publishing

Table of Contents

Table of Contents

Table of Contents 3

Acknowledgements 9

Chapter 1 - Introduction 10

Chapter 2 – The Maine Coon Cat 12

   History/Origin 12

   Myths Associated with Maine Coon Cats 14

   Pros and Cons of Owning a Maine Coon Cat 15

Chapter 3 – Appearance of the Maine Coon Cat 17

Chapter 4 – Psychology of the Maine Coon Cat 20

   Aggression 20

   Intelligence 21

   Curiosity 21

   Rubbing 22

   Body Language 22

   Vocals 23

   Panting 24

   House Soiling 24

   Poor Social Behaviour 25

Chapter 5 – Buying a Maine Coon 26

Table of Contents

From Your Neighbour/Friend 26

From a Rescue Center 26

From a Pet Store 26

From a Cat Breeder 27

How to Choose a Healthy Maine Coon 30

Pure Bred or Cross Bred and Why 30

Where to Buy 31

What Age to Buy and Why 35

One or More and Why 36

Male or Female and Why 37

Neutering/Spaying 37

Chapter 6 – How to Prepare for Your Maine Coon 40

What to Know Before You Buy 40

Essential Supplies 42

Non-Essential Supplies 44

Licensing 45

Micro-Chipping 46

Introducing Your Cat to Your Home 47

Introducing Your Cat to Other Pets 48

Introducing Your Cat to Family Members 48

Mistakes to Avoid 50

Table of Contents

Chapter 7 – Care for Your Maine Coon 53

    Basic Care.. 53

    Living Quarters... 55

    Grooming 55

    Transportation 58

    Exercises... 59

    Cat Toys.. 60

    Caring for a Pregnant Maine Coon Cat................................ 62

Chapter 8 – Feeding.. 66

    Nutrition... 66

    Kitten Nutrition Needs 68

    Adult Cat Nutrition Needs.. 68

    Old Cat Nutrition Needs 69

    The Right Food 69

    Feeding Program... 72

    Food Allergies.. 74

    What Not to Feed Your Cat... 75

    Cat Treats... 76

Chapter 9 – Training 78

    Cat Training... 78

    House Training 79

Table of Contents

   Behavioural Training 80

   Nocturnal Training 82

   Trick Training 83

   Dominance Training 83

   Command Training 83

   Leash Training 83

   Training Rules 84

Chapter 10 – Health 85

   Maine Coon Cat Health 85

   Common Illnesses/Diseases 85

   Signs of Illness 112

   When to Visit a Vet 114

   The Veterinarian 115

   How to Find a Vet 116

   Cat Insurance 117

Chapter 11 – Vaccinations 120

   What is a Vaccine? 120

   Safety of Vaccines 120

   Kitten Vaccination 121

   Adult Cat Immunization 121

   Core Cat Vaccines 121

Table of Contents

Non-Core Cat Vaccines.. 123

Chapter 12 – Costs..125

Chapter 13 – Caring for Your Aging Maine Coon....................130

What is aging?... 130

Psychological & Behavioural Changes...................................... 130

Health Challenges in Old Cats... 132

Chapter 14 – What to Do with an Old Maine Coon.................134

Cat Rescue Centre 134

Euthanasia 135

Home Care 136

Body Disposal 137

Cremation 137

Taxidermy 137

Desiccation.. 138

Resin Preservation 138

Post-Disposal Period 138

How to Cope with Your Maine Coon Cat's Death 139

Replacing Your Dead Maine Coon Cat................................... 139

Chapter 15 – Becoming a Maine Coon Cat Breeder 141

Who is a Breeder?... 141

Table of Contents

Things to Note *141*

General Breeding Information *143*

Building a Cattery *145*

Chapter 16 – International & National Cat Organizations, Associations and Clubs **148**

Conclusion **154**

Acknowledgements

I wish to convey special thanks to my family members who gave me the time and space I needed to write this book.

I would also like to pay special thanks to my friends and colleagues whose input proved valuable in obtaining all the necessary information I needed to develop the book.

Special thanks to the following organizations/associations for their valuable support;

The American Cat Fanciers Association (CFA)
America Pet Products Association
Cat Owners Association of Western Australia
The International Cat Association (TICA)
The Governing Council of the Cat Fancy (UK)
American Animal Hospital Association (AAHA)
Worldwide Pet Owners Association
The South African Cat Council
The Winn Feline Association
Feline Council of South Australia
The Governing Council of the Cat Fancy of South Australia (GCCFSA)
The Maine Coon Breeders and Fanciers' Association (MCBFA)
United Maine Coon Cat Association (UMCCA)
Cat Fanciers' Federation (CFF)
Maine Coon Cat Club (MCCC) – (UK)
Maine Coon Breed Society (UK)
Canadian Cat Association

Chapter 1 - Introduction

I have lived with both pets and farm animals for a very long time, a valuable opportunity that has given me a lot of experience in dealing with and handling both pets and farm animals.

My parents used to live in a remote rural area where they kept pets and reared livestock since I was born. I particularly got very interested in our pets that included three different dog breeds and four cat breeds. The cats were particularly of great interest to me and still are. This interest set me up for a long journey of interacting with cat breeders from across the world, breeders from whom I have learnt a lot relating to different cat breeds.

Of all cat breeds, the Maine Coon cat captured my attention to a point where the cat is now one of my favorite cats. I indeed have two of them as pets and can authoritatively claim to be in a good position to introduce it to cat lovers and others interested in having the cat as a pet.

The Maine Coon cat is one of the cat breeds that I have taken my time to carefully research on. With a very interesting history, this breed of cat has come a long way and is one of the best cat breeds to have at home as a pet, at least from my personal experience.

This breed of cat is only second to the Persian and Exotic breed of cats in terms of popularity, at least going Cat Fancier's Association records. It is therefore highly possible that established cat breeders have the breed in their catteries.

Maine Coon kitten and cat prize vary and depends on several factors. Some of the factors include breeder location, whether a kitten or cat's family tree is a "show" or "pet" line. In general

Chapter 1 - Introduction

breeder prices for pedigree Maine Coon kittens is between $400 and $800 (£290 and £590). Breeder price for an adult Maine Coon cat is between $800 and $1000 (£590 and £740).

You can also opt to buy a Maine Coon kitten or cat from a cat rescue center or shelter where price for kittens range between $200 and $600 (£150 and £445) while that of cats is between $500 and $800 (£370 and £590).

Chapter 2 – The Maine Coon Cat

History/Origin

Origin of Maine Coon cat is shrouded in many theories. It is however generally agreed that the breed is native to America. The breed is indeed referred to as the American Longhair.

One of the theories that attempt to indicate the origin of the breed relates to Marie Antoinette, once the Queen of France. Theory has it that while planning to escape France with the help of Captain Samuel Clough, she loaded the captain's ship with her six Turkish Angora cats, which were part of her valuable possessions. She was however captured before escaping and executed. Meanwhile, Captain Clough sailed off, making it possible for the cats on board to set foot on American soil in Wiscasset, Maine, where they mated with local American cats, giving rise to the modern Maine Coon cat.

Another theory on origin of Maine Coon cat breeds relates to one Captain Charles Coon who used to keep long-haired cats on his ship for the purpose of controlling rodents. Theory has it that Coon's cats would exit the ship whenever the ship docked in New England ports upon which they mated with local American feral cats that later gave birth to long-haired kittens, kittens that were later referred to as Coon's cats.

Although the exact origin of the Maine Coon remains unclear, it is generally believed that the breed came about due to mating between local American feral cats and long-haired foreign cats that came to American soil on-board ships. This gives credence to the theory that the breed came about from natural breeding between local feral cats and Captain Charles Coon's cats.

Chapter 2 - The Maine Coon Cat

With their long hair and strong build, the so called Captain Charles Coon's cats became very popular with local residents of Maine who kept them as working cats. Their popularity saw one Mrs. Fred Brown enter the breed in the first North American cat show held at the Madison Square Garden in 1895. The female cat emerged victorious, winning the silver collar and a medal with the silver collar later bought by the Cat Fanciers Association (CFA) Foundation. The collar still remains housed at CFA's Central Office, Jean Baker Rose Memorial Library.

The beginning of the 20th century saw a rapid decline of Maine Coon cats in the USA. This was due to introduction of such other long-haired cat breeds as the Persian. The last of Maine Coon cats to be entered in a cat show was at a cat show held in Portland, Oregon after which the breed became very rare. The breed was eventually declared extinct in early 1950s.

Fortunately, a few cat owners had still maintained their Maine Coon cats, allowing the breed to exist. This saw establishment of The Central Maine Coon Cat Club (CMCC) by Alta Smith and Ruby Dyer who embarked on a vigorous campaign to popularize the breed once again. The club held several cat shows and exhibitions in different locations across the USA. The club eventually created the first breed standard for the Maine Coon cat, giving the breed another opportunity to strive.

CMCC's campaigns saw re-emergence of the Maine Coon cat breed, making it popular in USA homes. The breed was once again exhibited in cat shows held across the US. Even so, the breed was not recognized by the CFA and therefore could not be entered in championship competitions. It was not until May 1975 that CFA finally recognized the breed by granting it provisional status. CFA eventually granted the breed full championship status in May 1976.

The period after 1976 has seen the Maine Coon cat breed become very popular in many homes across the USA from where the

Chapter 2 - The Maine Coon Cat

breed has been exported to other regions of the world. Cat breeders from across the world have taken in the breed, popularizing further. The year 1985 was a good year for the breed. This was when the state of Maine named the breed its official state cat. Maine Coon cat's popularity, at least in the USA has seen it occupy the third position behind the Persian and the Exotic cat breeds in terms of popularity.

Myths Associated with Maine Coon Cats
Like with other breeds of cat and other pets, there are several myths associated with the Maine Coon cat breed. Most of the breed's myths relate to its origin.

One myth goes that the breed came about by chance due to mating between American semi-wild domesticated cats and raccoons. This myth is misplaced because it is simply impossible for mating between the two to bring forth a kitten, at least in terms of genetics.

The other popular Maine Coon cat myth goes that the breed came about as a result of breeding between an American wild cat and a domestic cat. This myth cannot hold considering appreciating the fact that the Maine Coon breed would have been there long before arrival of other cat breeds.

Another myth that has come to be believed by many is that Maine Coon was domesticated from the wild. Many who hold on to this myth point to the cat's hairy nature and strong build. On the contrary, the Maine Coon cat is a pure domestic cat. Its hairy nature and strong muscles are genetically necessary to enable the cat to cope with the harsh weather and terrain found in Maine from where the breed is generally accepted to have originated from.

Chapter 2 - The Maine Coon Cat

Pros and Cons of Owning a Maine Coon Cat

Pros

The Maine Coon cat is one of the best cat breeds that you can have at home as a pet. It brings into a home an incredible beauty and calm that every home owner deserves. Despite of its huge size, the cat does not dominate a room in any way. It instead chooses to remain calm. It is the breed's calmness that has earned it such name tags as "the gentle cat" and "greeters of the world". Furthermore, it is very people-oriented and will want to be close to you so long as you are available.

Unlike most cat breeds, the Maine Coon cat breed is neither hyperactive nor a climber. In addition to remaining calm, it chooses to avoid anything to do with heights, instead choosing to remain very gentle either sleeping on the sofa, your lap or watching what you do.

Maine Coon cats do not need as much attention as dogs do. Furthermore, they turn out to be great entertainers. They literally entertain themselves with cat toys, boxes and water. When not entertaining themselves, Maine Coons spend most of their day napping.

The Maine Coon cat is the best cat you can have as a pet when it comes to love, affection and loyalty. The cat in particular remains loyal to its owner who it will try to do anything to appease.

The fact that the cat is very people-oriented makes it the best cat you can have as a companion. It is particularly good with senior citizens since it can be trained to perform light tasks. It is indeed very receptive to training and is very good at following given instructions.

Chapter 2 - The Maine Coon Cat

Cons

Maine Coon cats are huge. Its big size can be very intimidating to small children and other small pets at home. Although it is generally a gentle cat, it can turn to be very dominating when not properly trained.

The cat has long and thick hair. It therefore sheds big clumps of hair all over the place. It therefore requires regular grooming, which can be a burden to one who is not prepared to engage in grooming it on a regular basis.

Maine Coon cats are highly predisposed to Hypertrophic Cardiomypathy (HCM), which is a heart disease. Maintaining the cat through regular veterinary check-ups can turn out to be both expensive and time consuming.

The pros of the Maine Coon cat certainly outweigh its cons. This is something that I can vouch for considering that I have not only researched on the breed extensively but own two of them.

Chapter 3 – Appearance of the Maine Coon Cat

General Appearance
Looking at a Maine Coon cat is similar to looking at a small dog that is sturdy and bulky with big paws. The cat features a rectangular body and large bone structure. Its physical features are very appropriate considering that it is a cat used to harsh winter conditions. Its water-resistant fur is particularly long, thick and shaggy. It features a long, bushy and strong tail that allows it to remain afloat when in water. The tail is long enough to a point where it is able to curl it around its shoulders or face for warmth. Its large hairy paws have traditionally aided the cat to walk on snow.

Head
Maine Coon features a medium-sized head. The muzzle appears squared and can be broad in males. The cat has high cheek bones with the nose medium in length.

Chapter 3 - Appearance of the Maine Coon Cat

Body
Maine Coon's body is large with the chest being broad. The overall body is muscular. The body is long and rectangular in appearance.

Coat
Although the cat's hair is characteristically long, the length is not uniform over the whole body. Its hair in particularly is shorter on the head and shoulders and increases gradually toward the rest of the body. The hair is very soft and lies very close to the body.

Colour
You can find a Maine Coon cat in such solid colors as black, white, blue cream and red. The Maine Coon is also available in over seventy five colour combinations including shaded white, shaded silver, blue-silver, cameo, cream cameo, silver tabby, brown tabby and blue tabby among many others.

Body Weight
The Maine Coon cat breed develops very slowly. A Maine Coon cat takes between four and five years to attain its full size. This is when it attains body length of up to 120 cm (47 inches) including the tail, which can measure about 36 cm (14 inches). A mature cat stands at between 10 and 16 cm (3 – 6 inches).

A male Maine Coon cat weighs between 7 and 12 kg (15 Ibs – 26 Ibs). Females weigh less, which can be between 5 and 9 kg (11 Ibs – 19 Ibs).

Temperament
Maine Coon cats are easy-going, gentle and people-oriented. They are one of the most loving cats. They form a very strong attachment with their owners. They get along very well with children and such other pets as different cat breeds and dogs.

Chapter 3 - Appearance of the Maine Coon Cat

Unlike some cat breeds, the Maine Coon cat breed is not demanding. It prefers human companionship instead of seeking for attention. It also prefers to sit or lie next to you instead of on your lap. The breed particularly likes water not to swim in but for play. This is one cat breed that enjoys play activities right into old age.

Although big in size, the Maine Coon has a very soft voice. It communicates by producing different sounds; meowing, purring, cheeping and trilling. One unique habit you are most likely to note about the cat is that of giving you a soft head butt.

Maine Coons are traditionally cats used to cold climate. They however thrive in all climatic conditions so long as they are kept indoors.

Chapter 4 – Psychology of the Maine Coon Cat

Aggression

The Maine Coon cat can simply be described as a cat with good character. It has a way of winning over even the most hardened person. It is gentle, playful and very affectionate.

The cat's personality does not in any way mean that it cannot be aggressive, in which case there is acquired and genetic aggression. Like any other feline, a Maine Coon can acquire aggression depending on how it has been brought up. A feline brought up in a harsh environment where it is subjected to constant mistreatment will naturally develop aggression as one way of defending itself.

Genetic aggression is very different. By their nature, Maine Coon cats are working cats and very good at hunting. They therefore tend to bring into play their hunting skills, which involve biting and clawing. The cat is however very receptive to training and can easily be trained not to be aggressive during play.

Cats are by their nature territorial beings. A Maine Coon will naturally mark the house as its territory and will defend the same through aggression when it threatened. Territorial aggression is usually with male Maine Coons, which they exhibit when another male cat is introduced. This is when the cat hisses, growls and spits. Separating a new pet from the cat turns out to be the most effective way of preventing controlling aggression, which eventually wears off as the cat gets used to the newcomer.

There are also times when a Maine Coon cat can be aggressive when under threat. This mostly happens when confronted with a

Chapter 4 - Psychology of the Maine Coon Cat

larger pet or animal within the home. The cat can easily re-direct its aggression towards the owner, in which case biting and clawing is highly possible.

Intelligence

Intelligence here refers to your Maine Coon's capacity to solve problems, learn and adapt to its surrounding. From the onset, Maine Coons adapt to new environments very easily so long as they are well treated and provided for. Kittens in particular get used to new environments very fast because they set out to explore any new environment they are introduced to.

The Maine Coon is one of the most intelligent cats. This is one reason why they are very efficient at hunting. The cat easily gets accustomed to routines at home and will do everything to please its master by sticking to a set routine. It is also because of their high intelligence that Maine Coons are easy to train.

The cat has very high memory, which contributes to its level of intelligence. The play activities the cat engages in do not only serve as its way of life or behavior; it learns a lot from such activities and it is only appropriate that you have many but different cat toys. Play activities help them in exercising their minds and in honing their natural skills.

Curiosity

Living with a Maine Coon is similar to having a three-year old child at home. Always innocent, willful and charming, the cat remains inquisitive and curious all the time. It strives to know what its master is up to with the aim of helping where it can or to do the same. This cat's curiosity can however be very damaging when the cat is not properly trained. A Maine Coon cat can decide to re-arrange a room when it feels like, in which case it may end up damaging anything within its vicinity.

Chapter 4 - Psychology of the Maine Coon Cat

Rubbing

Like cats in the wild, the Maine Coon cat has the natural instinct of marking its territory within the house and everything therein. This is very common with a male cat that rubs itself on furniture, walls and on your legs. This is a natural behaviour that should not be of serious concern. While rubbing itself against everything in sight, your Maine Coon cat releases pheromones through its scent glands located on its tail and other parts of the body. You have the option of neutering/spaying the cat in case this behaviour is on the extreme.

Body Language

Of all signs and signals, the signs and signals that cats send out through their body language are very important. Your Maine Coon's body posture at any given time serves as an indication of its state of mind. The cat will behave in a particular manner when it is in a relaxed position. Whether lying down or sitting, it will most likely have its legs bent, the tail loosely wrapped around its shoulders or head. These will be accompanied by normal breathing.

There are times when your Maine Coon cat will exhibit alert body posture in which case it will lye down on its belly with its back horizontal. Although its breathing may be normal, it will have its legs either bent or extended with the tail curved toward the back. It may twitch its tail from one side to another. This is usually behaviour of a cat focused on something such as a live prey.

Tensed cats usually present body posture in such a way that the back remains lower than their upper body while lying down. Your Maine Coon cat may be moving forward or backwards with its hind legs bent and the front legs extended. The tail may be curled downwards or curled up. This is usually a clear sign of aggression.

Your Maine Coon cat and a female one in particular will once in a while present a body posture where the back of its body is the

Chapter 4 - Psychology of the Maine Coon Cat

only part of the body that remains visible with the front part less visible. This can happen when it is lying down on its belly or when in a standing position. The breathing in most cases is usually fast with the tail very close to the body in a curled position. This is usually a sign of anxiety. It can also be a sign that your cat is on heat in case it is not spayed.

You should find it easy to know when your cat is either terrified or fearful. It will most likely be in a crouched position on its paws with its entire body shaking. The tail will remain close to its body, the tail curled and close to the body. Although big in size, it will try to increase its size further as a way of fending off the threat.

Your Maine Coon cat will not only serve you as a pet and a companion; it will also serve to warn you of possible dangers within the house or compound. Any body language sign or signal your cat sends out needs immediate attention since it may notice a threat long before you do.

Vocals
There are those who refer to the Maine Coon as the "talking cat". They are not wrong. Maine Coons are known to produce different sounds with a very soft voice. They literally sound as if they talk. Maine Coons have a very distinct voice. Unlike most cats, a Maine Coon cat will not welcome you with a simple meow. It will purr, meow and trill, which most people think to be a way of describing to you how its day has been.

Maine Coons are generally not vocal and it is very important that you pay attention whenever they produce any sound. Excessive meowing usually means it is in need of something. Loud, high-pitched frantic and repeated meowing is usually a sign of danger or distress. You will need to respond to such calls immediately since your Maine Coon will be in dire need of help.

Chapter 4 - Psychology of the Maine Coon Cat

Panting

Although cats generally do not pant like dogs, there are times when your Maine Coon cat will pant. This will most likely be when travelling in a car, when stressed, when anxious and when on heat among other situations. You will however take note of excessive panting as the same may be a sign of illness.

House Soiling

House soiling is the most disturbing behaviour you will most likely observe your cat engage in. House soiling simply means urinating or defecating all over instead of using a provided litter box.

While it is perfectly normal for your cat to urinate (spray) outside its litter box, defecating outside the litter box can be because of other reasons. Your Maine Coon cat will most likely spray outside its litter box as one way of marking its territory. Unlike regular urination, your cat will spray while standing and probably with one leg raised instead of squatting. Spraying becomes common when you have several cats in the house in which case the dominant cat (usually a male) marks its territory.

Urination and defecation outside the litter box can be because of several reasons one of which is a medical problem. Any inflammation of your cat's urinary tract will cause frequent and some times painful urination. Because it is most likely to associate the pain it experiences with the litter box, it will avoid the same. The other reason may be because of the urgency to urinate when the litter box is in a different room.

Another reason for house soiling can simply be aversion. Your Maine Coon cat may find the litter box unsuitable for several reasons including bad odour, high-sided litter box, dirty litter box, distasteful litter box and inappropriate location of the litter box.

House soiling can be very traumatizing. It is therefore very important that you take all necessary measures to find out why your cat engages in this form of behaviour. It is always recommended that you take your cat to a vet for assessment in case there is no apparent reason for house soiling.

Poor Social Behaviour

Gentle, sociable, friendly and affectionate, Maine Coon cats rarely exhibit poor social behaviour. A Maine Coon is playful particularly where there is water and will want you to engage in play. Although very cautious in the presence of a stranger, it quickly gets used to the stranger with whom it will also want to engage in play. Your cat may at times simply want to lie down and rest, in which case it will cuddle on the sofa besides you or be alone in a secluded corner.

Chapter 5 – Buying a Maine Coon

The fact that the Maine Coon breed is one of the oldest breeds of cat means that you are likely to find it in many homes around the world. This also means that you are most likely to find a Maine Cat cross breed instead of pure breed. There are however several ways through which you can have a Maine Coon cat.

From Your Neighbour/Friend
This is the easiest way to acquire a Maine Coon kitten or cat. You can have a neighbour with kittens, in which case you may buy or simply receive one or several for free. This way of acquiring cats or any other pet for that matter is however not recommended for several reasons. First, the kitten you buy may not necessarily be pure breed. Secondly, you may acquire kittens with serious health problems.

From a Rescue Center
You are likely to find either a general cat rescue center or a dedicated Maine Coon rescue center depending on your location. While some of these centers offer rescued Maine Coons for adoption, others sell them off to obtain necessary funds for maintaining other rescued pets. Gaining possession of a Maine Coon from a recue center may not be appropriate because caretakers are not necessarily knowledgeable about them. This simply means that you will not receive the necessary advice on how to maintain your cat in the most recommended way.

From a Pet Store
There are dedicated pet stores that offer Maine Coon kittens and cats for sale. While some of such stores are breeder outlets, others are operated by individual owners who may not have sufficient

Chapter 5 - Buying a Maine Coon

information regarding the breed. You may therefore consider buying a kitten or cat from a breeder.

From a Cat Breeder

The popularity of the Maine Coon breed across the world has made it possible for establishment of many catteries that cater for the increasing demand for the same. Some of the established catteries have a very long history having been in the business of breeding other cat breeds for many years.

Well established breeders around the world are members of different organization and associations. Such organizations/associations include The International Cat Association (TICA), American Cat Fanciers Association (CFA), The Governing Council of the Cat Fancy (UK), South African Cat Council, Feline Council of South Australia, United Maine Coon Cat Association (UMCCA), The Maine Coon Breeders and Fanciers' Association (MCBFA), Cat Fanciers Federation (CFF), Maine Coon Cat Club (MCCC)-(UK), Maine Coon Breed Society (UK) and Canadian Cat Association among other organizations/associations.

Different Maine Coon cat owners in specific regions and locations in the world also have formed their own clubs for the purpose of sharing information about the breed.

How to Choose a Breeder

Buying a Maine Coon from either a general cat breeder or a specialized Maine Coon cat breeder provides for several benefits. Although buying from a breeder can be expensive depending on your location, the quality of a kitten or cat you buy is no doubt high. This is because breeders put in a lot of effort in ensuring that a kitten or cat you buy is not only properly vaccinated but is also free of common Maine Coon cat health problems.

Chapter 5 - Buying a Maine Coon

Although buying a Maine Coon from a breeder is highly recommended, it is very important that you choose a breeder carefully. Doing so makes it possible for you to buy a healthy cat.

One of the most things you need to look into is whether or not a breeder is a member of a national, regional or international cat association. Such breeders do adhere to code of ethics formulated by associations. A reputable breeder should be available for consultation when it becomes necessary long after purchasing your cat.

It is also very important that you ascertain whether or not a breeder you plan to buy from has all the requisite certifications and in particular, certifications relating to screening out of genetic health problems.

Perhaps a good way to choosing the right breeder lies in consulting with your local veterinarian who is in a better position to know local reputable Maine Coon cat breeders.

Questions to Ask
The most important thing to do when visiting a cat breeder with the aim of buying a kitten or cat is to ask questions. A reputable breeder should be willing to help you understand a Maine Coon kitten or cat. Most reputable breeders allow you to see the whole Maine Coon litter before you choose one or several to buy.

Your initial observation about a kitten or kitten should from the first instance inform you on a kitten's or cat's appropriateness. In addition to a cattery's overall cleanliness, a kitten or cat you are interested in should look healthy and clean. In particular, a kitten's or cat's hips and backbone need to be well covered. Likewise, a kitten or cat must not exhibit a pot belly, which is in most cases is a sign of worm infestation.

A kitten's or cat's eyes should not be bright and free of any sign of discharge. You need to examine the ears, which should not have any signs of particles. Presence of black particles in the ears is in most cases a sign of flea infestation.

There are a number of critical questions that you need to ask a breeder before you make any financial commitment. Asking some or all of questions relating to the following will be of great benefit to you.

Experience
You need to choose a breeder with some years of experience in breeding cats and in particular Maine Coon cats. It is also important to ascertain whether or not a breeder participates in cat shows. Breeders who participate in cat shows do not only have the experience but valuable knowledge as well, knowledge that will benefit you as the breeder will certainly share the same with you.

Breeding Style
It is very important that you ascertain a breeder's breeding style before you buy. A knowledgeable breeder will normally adopt a breeding style that addresses Maine Coon cat's health problems. Buying from such a breeder ensures that you buy a kitten or cat with very minimal health issues to deal with.

Vaccinations
Like with all other animals, it is good to ascertain if a breeder's Maine Coon kittens or cats receive the requisite vaccinations before they are sold off. It is very important that you only buy a vaccinated kitten or cat to reduce veterinary costs.

Guarantees
Although not offered by all Maine Coon cat breeders, buying a kitten or cat with health guarantee can be very beneficial to you. A cat that you buy can fall ill within days of buying and it is only appropriate that you have some level of guarantee.

Chapter 5 - Buying a Maine Coon

Certification
In addition to a breeder's certification, it is good to ascertain whether or not parents of a kitten you are about to buy are certified. This simply means that a kitten whose parents are certified will not be at risk of suffering genetic health conditions.

These are just a few of the many critical questions that you need to ask a breeder. Doing so makes it possible for you to buy a quality kitten or cat that is easy to maintain in terms of veterinary costs. You may however need to realize that finding a specialized Maine Coon cat breeder since most turn out to be general cat breeders.

How to Choose a Healthy Maine Coon
Whether buying a Maine Coon kitten or cat, identifying a healthy one to buy should not be a problem. In addition to physical observation and examination, the other way to ascertain a kitten's health status is to see the kitten's parents. Maine Coon cats are generally playful, which should also be evident in their kitten.

Undertaking a pre-purchase examination is also very important. A reputable cat breeder will normally allow you to visit with a qualified veterinarian for such examination. A vet should be in a position to perform a number of routine tests including the cat's general blood work, viral tests, stool/urine analysis and general physical examination.

Pure Bred or Cross Bred and Why
This is one of the most important decisions you have to make when planning to by a cat. Like with other cat breeds, you will come across purebred and crossbred Maine Coon kittens. However, breeders do restrict themselves to selling pure bred Maine Coon kittens or cats.

Buying a purebred Maine Coon kitten or cat can be beneficial to you considering that you end up with a cat whose personality and characteristics you know perfectly well. Furthermore, buying a

Chapter 5 - Buying a Maine Coon

purebred cat makes it possible for you to deal with known health challenges that the Maine Coon breed is susceptible to. Although crossbred Maine Coon cats do face similar health challenges as purebred, theirs may be complicated to deal with because of genetic alterations. The cost of purebred Maine Coon kittens and cats is usually higher than that of crossbreds.

Where to Buy

Please note I have not bought cats from all these companies so make sure to check them out before you buy from them.

Enchantacats (www.enchantacats.com)

This cattery is located in a 14-acre land in Gold County, California. The facility has both indoor and outdoor cat breeding equipment. Within the facility are dogs that kittens are introduced to with the aim of bonding as part of their training.

Kittens from this facility are known to be well trained, healthy and very active. The facility is registered by TICA and CFA. This is one of catteries that provide buyers with sales agreement, baby blankets and grooming products. Maine Coon kittens sold are usually screened for FIV and FIP.

Karmacoons (www.karmacoons.com)

This is a small home-based cattery located in Orlando, Florida. All the cattery's cats are usually entered into cat shows and are registered with both TICA and CFA. Kittens bought from this cattery are known to bond very well with other cat breeds and pets. This is so because they are raised in a home environment where they constantly play with children and dogs.

This cattery only sells Maine Coon kittens that have already received requisite vaccinations with health certificate issued.

Chapter 5 - Buying a Maine Coon

Likewise, all the cattery's kittens are usually screened for HCM before being sold off.

MaineSail (www.mainesailonline.com)

This cattery is located in Atlanta, Georgia. It is registered by TICA, ACFA and CFA. The owners also have other catteries in such other locations as Missouri, Iowa and Minnesota. In addition to breeding Maine Coon cat breed, the cattery also participates in Maine Coon cat championship shows both across the US and other regions of the world.

Long Beach Cattery (www.longbeachcattery.co.uk)

This is a small cattery located in New Forest, Hampshire in the UK. It is owned by Pamela Nunn who has been breeding cats for the last twenty five years. Nunn initially bred Burmese cats before switching to Maine Coons. Her cattery is registered by GCCF and sells socialized and inoculated kittens.

Dracoonfly (www.dracoonfly.com)

This is a cattery located in Ledyard, Connecticut, USA. Registered by both TICA and CFA, the cattery has the motto of improving, preserving and protecting Maine Coon cat breed.

Kittens from this cattery are known to be highly social. This is because each kitten in the cattery is not only given a unique name that it gets used to but introduced to other cat breeds and dogs from a young tender age.

The cattery has adopted modern medical screening methods that eliminate unhealthy genes from the cattery. This simply means that kittens sold by the cattery are not susceptible to hereditary diseases/health conditions associated with the Maine Coon cat breed.

Chapter 5 - Buying a Maine Coon

In addition to screening for known diseases/health conditions, the cattery also neuters/spays kittens before they are sold off, unless a client wishes to buy un-neutered/spayed kittens.

The cattery has over the years earned several awards in Maine Coon cat championship shows including CFA's Cattery of Excellence and TICA's Outstanding Cattery awards.

Barncat Classic Maine Coons (www.classicmainecoons.com)

This is a cattery located in Southeastern part of Massachusetts in the US. Unlike most Maine Coon cat breeders, the breeder breeds Maine Coons as a hobby and is registered by both TICA and CFF.

The breeder breeds healthy Maine Coon kittens in different colours without altering breed standard. The breeder's breeding style is in making use of different Maine Coon breed genes to produce Maine Coon kittens with diverse characteristics. It is through this style that the breeder has been able to produce Maine Coon kittens with attractive body structure, good temperament and great facial expression.

Unlike most Maine Coon breeders, this breeder has adopted free-range breeding style, meaning that cats and kittens are left to roam around within a protected area. This style has proved to be very beneficial to the Maine Coon since the breed requires a lot of fresh air.

Spirithillcats (www.spirithillcats.com)

This cattery is located in Elbert County, East Denver, US. It is a small home-based cattery that has earned the reputation of breeding healthy Maine Coons with good temperament and discipline. The cattery is registered by both CFA and TICA. The breeder is a regular participant in many Maine Coon cat championship shows organized by the two organizations.

Chapter 5 - Buying a Maine Coon

This is one breeder who has studied cat breeding and is therefore a qualified cat breeder after having undertaken a Feline Genetics Course. The breeder screens for various diseases/health conditions before selling kittens off. Kittens bought from the cattery are therefore free from such diseases/health conditions as hip dysplasia, spinal muscular atrophy and hypertrophic Cardiomyopathy.

Koontahhdin Maine Coons (www.koontahdin.com)

This is a small home-based cattery located in Sudbury, Massachusetts in the US. Named after Mount Katahdin, which is highest peak in Maine from where the Maine Coon cat breed came from, the breeder breeds healthy Maine Coons with very good personality. The cattery is registered by both CFA and TICA and breeder participates in many Maine Coon cat championship shows organized by the two organizations.

All kittens sold by the breeder are usually sold after being neutered/spayed with a health certificate issued. Indeed all the cattery's kittens are usually screened for various diseases/health conditions before being sold off.

Rydalmaine Maine Coons (www.rydalmaine-maine-coons.co.uk)

This cattery is located in Peterborough, Cambridgeshire in the UK. The cattery is registered by both GCCF and TICA. This is a small family cattery with the family breeding Maine Coon purely as a hobby.

Because of its small size, the number of litters usually available is limited. Maine Coon cat lovers who intend buying from the cattery are required to make arrangements in good time to secure the same before they are born.

Chapter 5 - Buying a Maine Coon

Kizzacoons (www.kizzacoonsmainecoons.co.uk)

This is a small family-owned cattery located in Market Harborough in Leicestershire, UK. The cattery is registered by both TICA and FiFE. All the cattery's kittens are raised indoor and are therefore raised as indoor cats.

Because of how they are raised, the cattery's kittens are known to be highly social, obedient and of good character. Because of small size, only a few kittens are usually available at any given time for sale.

Supercoons (www.supercoonsmainecoons.com)

This is one of the few dedicated Maine Coon cat breeders in Australia. The breeder started breeding Maine Coons after relocating from South Africa in 2008, having been introduced to the breed in 2007. Although a teacher by profession, the breeder reserves quality time to her cattery, socializing with the kittens.

With the goal of breeding healthy, social and obedient Maine Coons, the breeder constantly engages a veterinarian to screen kittens for such diseases/health conditions as hip dysplasia, HCM, FeIV and FIV among other diseases/health conditions.

These are just a few breeders from whom you can buy Maine Coon kittens or cats. Because importing cats from a different country can not only be costly but very involving, it is always recommended that you first search for a breeder within your locality or region to buy from before looking elsewhere.

What Age to Buy and Why

This is one of the important decisions you need to make even before you visit a cat breeder with the aim of buying a Maine Coon cat. The age of your children at home is very critical. Although Maine Coons are generally fond of children, having young children at home may make it necessary for you to buy one aged two years and above. This will be a cat capable of understanding children.

Being a senior citizen makes it necessary to avoid buying Maine Coon kittens at all costs. This is because kittens can be very mischievous and troublesome. They need constant watch, a task you may not be comfortable performing. You may therefore need to buy one aged at least two years. Note that buying a much older cat may not be appropriate considering the fact that an old cat is already used to a specific routine and behaviour.

How much time you plan to spend with your cat is also a very important factor to consider. Buy a Maine Coon cat aged at least three years in case you will not be at home all the time, unless you plan to have someone at home on a regular basis.

You may consider buying a Maine Coon kitten if you take into consideration the element of training. Maine Coon breeders do offer kittens aged at least 15 weeks for sale. Although a kitten you buy will have received some level of basic training, you will still have the opportunity to offer the kind of training that suits your home and your preference.

One challenge that you may face when you buy a kitten is in determining its personality. The fact that you are not in a position to determine a kitten's personality at such a young age may make it necessary to buy a young but mature Maine Coon cat.

One or More and Why

The decision on whether to buy one, two or more Maine Coons depends on several factors one of which is resources. You may opt to buy two cats if you are financially capable of meeting their feeding, care, grooming and health needs. You also need to consider the amount of space you have in your house. Although you may be comfortable with only one, it would be ideal if you buy two for their own companionship.

Chapter 5 - Buying a Maine Coon

Male or Female and Why

Different people have different preferences when it comes to gender of a pet they plan to buy and the same applies to buying Maine Coons. While there are those who prefer male cats, there are also those comfortable with female cats.

The most important thing to note is that whether you choose to buy a male or a female Maine Coon, each gender has its pros and cons. Like with other male cats of other breeds, a male Maine Coon will roam in search of a female to mate with. Males also tend to mark their territory both indoors and outdoors, which creates an environment where cat fights may be the order of the day when you introduce another male cat or a different pet or in case there is another in your neighbourhood.

Likewise, a female Maine Coon will also roam in search of a mating partner when on heat. Note that a female Maine Coon like with other female cat breeds will come on heat regularly until such a time when it finds a mate, a period that can last up to 16 days. Female Maine Coons usually become sexually mature once they attain the age of between eight and ten months and you may not find it comfortable living with a female on heat considering that she will keep on calling day and night.

Such problems should not in any way deter you from owning either gender of Maine Coon cat. You can have your kitten or adult cat de-sexed before you bring him/her home. De-sexing is the procedure where cats and other animals are subjected to surgical routines that make them incapable of reproducing. De-sexing literally kills their sex drive. While de-sexing in male animals is professionally known as neutering, it is spaying for female animals.

Neutering/Spaying

Neutering in male animals including Maine Coons involves removal of the testes. This renders your cat sterile, which provides for several benefits. On the other hand, spaying in

Chapter 5 - Buying a Maine Coon

female animals including Maine Coon females involves removal of ovaries and uterus. There are cases where only the ovaries are removed. Like with neutering, spaying also provides for several benefits.

Advantages of Neutering/Spaying
Having your cat neutered or spayed can be beneficial to you in many ways. In addition to being a birth control method, neutering/spaying transforms your cat's general behaviour. A male Maine Coon cat that has been neutered will not only show reduced aggression tendencies; it will also change its mounting and urine spaying behaviour. Likewise, a female Maine Coon that has been spayed will show less aggression toward males due to reduction in levels of sex hormones.

One of the biggest advantages of having your Maine Coon cat neutered/spayed is in elimination of roaming. Female cats do produce into the air pheromones when they are on heat. Pheromones are chemical signals that attract male cats for mating. A natured cat does not react on sensing pheromones in the air and will therefore not roam in search for the cat on heat. On the other hand, a spayed female cat is incapable of releasing pheromones and will therefore not roam in search of a male.

The benefits of having your cat de-sexed are not restricted to behavioural changes. There are health benefits as well. Spaying a female Maine Coon cat relieves it of anxiety and stress she would otherwise have when on heat and denied the opportunity to mate. Note that a female cat on heat can remain in the same state for up to 16 days and is bound to be stressed without an opportunity to mate. The female's condition is even made worse by the fact that it is bound to come on heat again after about 14 days after the initial phase.

Like with other cat breeds, female Maine Coons are susceptible to mammary cancer, which is mainly caused by reproduction hormones.

Spaying reduces the risk of mammary cancer by between 30 and 50%. Spaying also reduces the risk of such health problems as reproduction tract tumours and other associated infections.

Another benefit that de-sexing your cat provides relates to amount of money you would incur in maintenance. The cost of maintaining a de-sexed cat is relatively lower compared to maintaining a cat that has not been subjected to the same.

When to Have Your Cat Neutered/Spayed
There is really no fixed age at which you can have your cat neutered or spayed. You only need to consult with your veterinarian to perform the necessary surgical operation. A trend that is now emerging is where breeders offer for sale neutered/spayed kittens and cats before selling them off, saving you from the cost and the trouble of looking for a veterinarian to perform the procedure.

Maine Coon breeders in the USA in particular neuter male kittens when they are about six months old. Some breeders neuter them when they are only four weeks old. Likewise, females are spayed when they are between five and eight months. Some breeders spay them when they are only three months of age. Contrary to a common belief, neutering/spaying kittens at such a tender age does not hinder their overall development. Neutering/spaying kittens is also beneficial since they have the opportunity to heal faster than when de-sexing is performed when they are mature. Apart from breeders, you can have your cat neutered/spayed by your local veterinarian.

Chapter 6 – How to Prepare for Your Maine Coon

What to Know Before You Buy
There are a number of things you need to know before you buy a pet or a Maine Coon cat as a pet for that matter. Knowing some of these things will make living with your cat not only easy but an enjoyable experience as well.

Buying a Maine Coon is similar to introducing a new member into your family. You will be obligated to treat your cat in the same way that you do to your family members. You therefore need to be prepared to cater for your cat's needs in terms of food, veterinary care, shelter, grooming and love.

Buying a cat is a life-long commitment. You need to be prepared to live with your cat for long. Note that although Maine Coons

Chapter 6 - How to Prepare for Your Maine Coon

---

have a general life span of about 118 years, they can actually live much longer depending on quality of life you subject them to.

Unlike many other cat breeds, Maine Coons are not attention seekers although are at times are. You will however need to spend a considerable amount of time with your cat. Furthermore, be prepared to be watched keenly. This is because your Maine Coon cat will watch everything that you do and do not be surprised to have a helping hand.

The Maine Coon breed is both an indoor and outdoor pet. Although it spends most time indoors, it occasionally ventures outdoors not only to play but to explore as well. It is therefore very important that both the indoor and outdoor environments are pet friendly.

Bring your cat home only when everything is in place. Do not bring the cat home before you have enough food supply and other essentials such as bowls and play toys.

Scratching is an innate characteristic of all cat breeds, Maine Coon breed included. Ensure that you have a scratch post strategically located for your cat's convenience. Although you will occasionally groom your cat, you need to note that it will also indulge in self-grooming most of the time. You will therefore need to make your cat used to a specific spot for grooming.

The most important thing you cannot ignore when you are about to bring your cat home is to cat-proof your house by establishing a safe room. Cat-proofing your house simply means making your house as secure as possible for the benefit of your cat. This you can do by removing or storing sharp objects that stand out. A safe room does not necessarily mean a room preserved for the cat. It simply refers to a specific location such as an ideal corner within one of the rooms that your cat will be trained to get used to as its "home".

Chapter 6 - How to Prepare for Your Maine Coon

Essential Supplies

There is serious need to prepare well long before you bring home your Maine Coon kitten or cat home. You will need to invest in a good number of items/equipments for the benefit of your pet. It is very important that you invest in high quality equipments that will serve you for reasonable time. It is not mandatory that you must spend money in buying some of the equipments. There is equipment that you can easily make at home in case you happen to be a DIY person. The following are some of the most essential items that you must have.

Cat Food

Food is the first item that you must have before you bring your kitten or cat home. However, not all food stuffs will do. You need to buy specially formulated cat food that will allow your cat to grow strong and healthy. It is important to note that cats require specific dietary nutrients and it is only appropriate that you buy food stuffs that contain such nutrients.

Specially formulated commercial cat foods are readily available from pet food stores and it is recommended that you check at your local pet store outlet for the same.

You will definitely find cat food in different forms. Like with dry food stuffs, dry cat foods contain limited moisture. They are in most cases sprayed with fat to make them palatable. They also contain added nutrition ingredients to replace vital nutrients destroyed during preparation.

Wet cat food stuffs are usually canned or in foil pouch form. There are also fortified vegetarian cat foods. Because cats are obligate carnivores, their vegetarian food is usually fortified with such ingredients as taurine and arachidonic acid, ingredients that cats are not in a position to synthesize from plants.

Chapter 6 - How to Prepare for Your Maine Coon

It is highly recommended that you buy dry, wet and vegan cat food stuffs to allow your cat have complete diet. It is also highly recommended that you buy cat food from reputable stockists who stock cat food brands of good reputation.

Food & Water Dishes
Your cat will definitely eat and it is only appropriate that you buy recommended cat food and water dishes. Just in the same way that you pay attention to colour and size of your dishes, you need to choose your cat food and water dishes carefully. Doing so will make it possible for your cat to enjoy eating and drinking.

Litter Box & Scoops
By natural instinct, your cat will dig and bury its waste. It is therefore very necessary that you buy an appropriate litter box filled with clean litter. You have the option of buying an open or enclosed litter box. Self-cleaning litter boxes have of late hit the market, which you may also consider buying.

Cat Furniture
Although full of energy and at times very playful, your cat will once in a while want to rest and catch a nap. Investing in a cat condo is therefore very appropriate. Alongside a condo should be a cat tree. A cat tree is very important because your cat will naturally want to scratch in order to sharpen its claws. Having a cat tree will save you from the agony of having your furniture scratched. An alternative to a cat tree is a cat scratching post in case you have limited space.

Cat Carrier
It is very important that you invest in a quality cat carrier. It becomes handy when you need to transport your cat to the vet or when travelling. A quality carrier should have enough room in which you can place a small cat condo.

Chapter 6 - How to Prepare for Your Maine Coon

Brush
Investing in a brush is important. This is because the Maine Coon cat sheds hair often and the brush will come in handy. You will also brush your cat to prevent development of hairballs.

Collar
This is one of the most important things you cannot afford not to have when you bring your Maine Coon cat or kitten home. This is because you never know when your cat will venture outdoors with the possibility of getting lost. A collar that you buy should have room for your cat's name, your name and address/contact.

Non-Essential Supplies

Although generally considered as non-essential cat supplies, some of the following items can be very important especially when you need to have an active, healthy and intelligent Maine Coon cat as a companion. Maine Coons are generally playful, which may make it necessary for you to invest in cat toys. Alternatively, consider using such readily available items as paper bags and cardboards when playing with your cat.

Although your cat will naturally scratch as one way of sharpening/cutting its claws, you may need to consider investing in a cat nail clipper for trimming its claws.

Feeding your cat dry, wet and vegetarian food stuffs should be enough to cleanse its teeth. You may however consider buying cat toothbrush and paste just to ensure that you cleanse its teeth well.

Chapter 6 - How to Prepare for Your Maine Coon

Licensing

Bringing a Maine Coon home as a pet is similar to enlarging your family. The breed indeed develops closeness and unique attachment to all family members and considers itself part of the family. This is one of the reasons why you need to license your cat. Licensing your cat is similar to buying insurance cover. Licensing it makes it easy for animal control officers to reach you in case your cat gets lost and is found.

The other reason why you need to license your cat relates to disease control. You give out vital information to animal control officers when you license your cat. Data captured during licensing benefits you in a great way. This is so because you will be contacted in case of newly availed vaccinations. More importantly, licensing your cat makes it easy for animal officers, cat breeders and animal health authorities to have vital statistics necessary for planning.

Different countries have different legislations that relate to pets including cats. There are countries where cat owners are not obligated to buy licenses for their cats but buy for dogs. There are also countries where licensing is compulsory for all pets. Cat licensing requirements and fees differ across the Unites States of America. While it is mandatory in such states as Los Angeles for dogs to be licensed, licensing is not required for cats.

Likewise, there are states where it is mandatory for cats to be licensed. In addition to licensing, cats must carry proper identification. In such states, licensing is by a County's relevant animal authority. There are also states where veterinarians are given the responsibility of licensing cats. This is so because cat licenses are meant to last for the duration of vaccination. Cat owners therefore find it easy to renew their cat licenses when returning their cats for vaccination.

Cat licensing is mandatory in the UK. In addition, your cat will need to have a cat tag. Cat licensing in the UK is the

Chapter 6 - How to Prepare for Your Maine Coon

responsibility of different authorities concerned with welfare of cats and other pets. However, most licenses are issued by local authorities at the local level. Cat owners can also buy licenses or renew their cat licenses at animal care centers.

It is important that you do not view licensing your cat as a legal requirement. View it as one of the most effective ways of protecting your cat. You also need to consider registering your Maine Coon cat with your local Maine Coon cat club or association if you happen to live in an area with an established cat club or association. This particularly applies in case you live in a jurisdiction where licensing of cats is not mandatory.

Micro-Chipping
Micro-chipping refers to the latest technology used in identifying lost animals and pets. Unlike externally attached Radio Frequency Identification tags commonly used to identify farm animals, micro-chipping involves implantation of a small Radio Frequency Identification chip just under a pet's skin.

You can have your Maine Coon cat micro-chipped. This is a service offered by veterinarians. You will have the chip implanted under your cat's skin at the back of its neck. This is the area with layers of connective tissue capable of holding the chip in place. Although use of micro-chips is not yet widespread, there are jurisdictions where you are obligated to have your cat or other pet micro-chipped.

There are several benefits that you derive from having your cat micro-chipped. From the onset, it becomes easy for animal control officers and animal shelter organizations to contact you in case your cat gets lost and is found. Having your cat micro-chipped is also beneficial to you considering the fact that cat or pet registries, veterinarians and trainers use micro-chips to identify pets under their care.

Chapter 6 - How to Prepare for Your Maine Coon

Micro-chipping is very important and it is not surprising that many breeders including Maine Coon cat breeders micro-chip their kitten/cats before selling them off. The chip contains all the information that you provide including your name, residence and contact information.

Introducing Your Cat to Your Home

Just in the same way that you take time to get used to a new environment, your cat will take some time to get used to your home. Your cat may not behave in a way you expect during the first few days. It will certainly not eat and behave as you expect.

Like with any cat breed, the Maine Coon breed is a territorial animal. This is why it is very important that you designate for it a room or space in your house. Your cat will naturally spend the first few days or weeks learning every sound and smell in its territory before venturing into other rooms. One of the most important things that your cat will learn is your body language and the tone of your voice. It is therefore very important that you take all these into account when communicating with your cat.

Your main task during the first few days should be to introduce your cat to its important tools. This is the time to introduce it to its litter box, feeding dishes, water dishes and furniture including scratching post. Maine Coons are very intelligent and therefore learn very fast. They follow minor instructions to the letter. This is also the right time to introduce one or two toys for play.

Introducing toys will make your cat get involved in play activities, which will go a long way in eliminating boredom. You will need to spend the first few days observing your cat with the aim of ascertaining its demands, which you will need to fulfill. The main point here is to make your cat feel as comfortable as possible. One thing you are most likely to observe is its act of hissing and growling at any new sound or movement. This is normal and should not be a concern.

Chapter 6 - How to Prepare for Your Maine Coon

Introducing Your Cat to Other Pets

Bringing your cat home when you already have other pets and in particular another cat can be a serious challenge. This is so because the resident cat already considers your home its territory and will not welcome another cat very easily. Unlike other cat breeds however, the Maine Coon breed is very receptive to other cats and pets. The challenge may be how to deal with the other cat or pet. To prevent such a scenario, it is always recommended that a cat you introduce should be of the opposite sex of the resident cat. Note that you will not be able to prevent cat fights even when both of them are de-sexed.

The easiest way to introduce your Maine Coon cat to other cat(s) and pets is to set them apart. You need to create a separate room or space for your new cat and let them bond naturally. Bringing in a new cat and housing them in the same room or space can be very problematic.

Introducing Your Cat to Family Members

Introducing your cat to family members and in particular to children the first time you bring it home is not recommended. Doing so can be stressful to the cat. It can actually feel very uncomfortable and take very long to get used to its new environment.

Chapter 6 - How to Prepare for Your Maine Coon

When to introduce your cat to family members depends on how fast it has got used to its room or space. While some cats take between two and four weeks to get accustomed and start interacting with family members, others take as little as few days.

It is recommended that you do not introduce your cat to several family members at the same time. Only one family member should venture into the cat's room or space with the aim of bonding with the cat. For easy bonding, a family member venturing into the cat's room or space should not stand but rather sit on the flow when communicating with the cat. Light touch is recommended for the cat to get used to the family member and build trust.

Maine Coons are generally inquisitive and will naturally walk slowly toward a family member they are not used to. It is therefore very important that a family member who ventures into the cat's room or space for the first time keeps his/her distance and let the cat walk towards him/her.

One rule of thumb that any new family member venturing into a cat's room or space for the first time is to avoid picking up the cat. Maine Coons are generally not lap cats and do not like to be carried around. They choose when to leap onto one's lap. Even so, a family member interacting with the cat for the first time should avoid picking up the cat. Family members also need to note that there are times when the cat will want to have its peace and will show this by hiding underneath its furniture or bed. It should simply be left alone when this happens.

There are several ways through which you can introduce your cat to other family members quickly. The first of these is for a family member venturing into the cat's room or space to engage the cat in play activities with use of toys. Bringing the cat small amounts of food is also another great way for your cat to bond with other family members.

Chapter 6 - How to Prepare for Your Maine Coon

Although Maine Coons get along well with other pets including dogs, it can still be a challenge to bring a Maine Coon to a home with a dog as another pet. It is always a good idea to keep your cat indoors in its room or space before you allow it to venture into other rooms or outdoors. Even so, it will be beneficial to keep the dog on a leash to allow the cat explore its new surrounding. You will need to give your cat room to approach the dog on its own terms. Because your cat will naturally approach the dog to sniff it, you will need to be prepared to act when necessary, just in case the dog is not welcoming.

The first few days or weeks upon bringing your cat home will be very involving and challenging. It is therefore very important that you create enough time to be at home most of the time to ensure that your cat remains comfortable as much as possible. The challenge eventually wears off once the cat gets used to its new environment, family members and other pets in the home.

Mistakes to Avoid

There are several serious mistakes that most new cat owners do that you need to avoid at all costs. Avoiding these mistakes goes a long way in helping your cat get used to its new environment fast enough.

One of the serious mistakes you need to avoid is to fail to make your home pet-friendly. You need to make your home pet-friendly by ensuring that all that your cat will need is in place before you bring it home. Create for your cat a special room or space. You also need to equip the room or space with all that the cat will need. These include litter box, cat furniture and food/water dishes among other vital equipment.

Maine Coons are people-oriented cats and one of the costly mistakes you need to avoid is to leave your cat alone for lengthy periods of time. Leaving your cat alone for a long time can easily drive it into developing a feeling of loneliness, increased anxiety

Chapter 6 - How to Prepare for Your Maine Coon

---

and undesired behaviour. Make it a point to have someone at home most of the time as your cat will need companionship.

Maine Coons are clever and highly intelligent cats. They are very receptive to training, which you need to embark on as early as possible. Although certain training aspects will definitely require a professional trainer, teaching your Maine Coon obedience commands should not be a problem. Ensure that your cat can positively respond to such minor commands as sit, stay and leave. A cat that follows commands will rarely develop untoward behaviour.

Every home has rules that family members are obligated to stick to and your home is no exception. As part of your family, do not fail to make your cat aware of simple rules particularly when it comes to feeding time. It cannot only be embarrassing but injurious for your cat to pounce on your hands when presenting it with food. You need to avoid such behaviour by getting your cat used to sitting before feeding. This is something that the rest of your family members must be aware of.

Another serious mistake you need to avoid is to give your cat too many treats. While treats are an effective way of rewarding your cat whenever it does something positive such as following instructions, giving too many treats negates the value of training. You need to use treats sparingly. Restrict dispensing of treats to those occasions when your cat does something extra.

One of the costly mistakes that new cat owners make is neglecting to socialize with their pets as much as possible. Like with dogs, failure to socialize with your cat makes it fearful and can easily develop aggressive behaviour. It is therefore appropriate to introduce your cat not only to family members but to your visitors as well.

Maine Coons are both indoor and outdoor pets. Apart from venturing outdoors for play, they also spend some time outdoors

Chapter 6 - How to Prepare for Your Maine Coon

for adventure. One of the mistakes you need avoid is to restrict your cat indoors. It is always good to take your cat out for walks, giving it an opportunity to climb trees, which is its nature. Doing so allows your cat to release pent-up energy that it would otherwise channel into undesirable behaviour.

A common mistake that most cat owners commit that you also need to avoid is failure to keep their cats mentally active. Many cat owners limit themselves to socializing with their cats, forgetting that keeping their cats mentally active is also beneficial. Like with other pets, cats kept without mental activity become easily bored. Engage in play activities using cat toys. Hide such toys and let your cat find them out.

Maine Coons are very adorable, which makes many of their owners commit one serious mistake; failure to punish their cats when they engage in untoward behavior. Because physical punishment is likely to instill fear in your cat, consider using a harsh tone when communicating and expressing your disapproval for a behavior that does not impress you.

These are just a few of the mistakes you need to avoid if you need to have a well behaved and obedient Maine Coon as a pet. Failure on your part will simply mean having a pet that you cannot control, which will be a recipe for serious problems at home.

Chapter 7 – Care for Your Maine Coon

Basic Care
Like with all cats, your Maine Coon depends on you for everything including basic care. Although your cat is independent to some extent, you are still obligated to provide it with suitable and healthy food, shelter, veterinary care, training and love. It is only with appropriate basic care that you can be able to develop a strong and rewarding relationship with your cat.

Apart from such necessities as food and shelter, proper hygiene is mandatory as part of basic care. Your cat needs to be in a clean environment at all times. Do ensure that all equipment including litter box, food/water dishes, playing toys and the room remain clean all the time. Cats are generally clean pets and do not be surprised when your cat avoids the litter box, feeding and its room when you fail to maintain good hygiene standard.

Basic care also involves your cat's safety. Being an indoor and outdoor cat, you need to know where your cat is at all times. This is when cat collars and ID tags become useful just in case your cat wanders off and gets lost.

Just in the same way that you and your family members visit your physician for regular check-ups, your cat also needs to visit a vet for regular check-ups. You do not need to wait for your cat to show signs of illness to take it to a vet. It is during such check-ups that minor signs of illnesses can be diagnosed and proper treatment administered. This is one of the most important basic care routines that you cannot ignore when you need to have a healthy Maine Coon cat as a pet.

Chapter 7 - Care for Your Maine Coon

Closely related to regular check-ups is feeding. Failure to feed your cat on nutritious food can easily lead to cat medical problems. You need to avoid the practice by some cat owners who feed their cats on dog food. Cat nutritional requirements differ in a big way from dog nutrition needs and feeding your cat on dog food simply denies your cat vital nutritional supplies. Grooming is a very important part of your cat's basic care. You still need to groom your Maine Coon cat even though it indulges in self-grooming. Doing so is very effective in reducing development of hairballs and matting. In addition to grooming, you also need to clip your cat's claws.

Training your cat is a very important part of basic care. By their nature, cats generally know how to do their own things, which, regrettably, may not be proper. Training your cat from the earliest opportunity goes a long way in preventing such habits as jumping on the kitchen counter, scratching the couch and eating plants. Note that it is through training that your cat comes to learn about applicable house rules. Although cats generally know how to entertain themselves, a male Maine Coon cat in particular can be very playful. It is therefore very important that you regularly engage your cat in play activities by use of cat toys and other suitable items. Engaging your cat in play activities provides for valuable benefits including strengthening your relationship. Furthermore, playing with your cat on a regular basis provides it with both physical strength and mental stimulation it so much needs.

There is nothing great and valuable as giving your cat proper basic care right from the time you bring it home. Giving your cat basic care can indeed be beneficial to you since you will prevent common cat diseases that can otherwise be costly when you have to take your cat to a vet for treatment. It is also by giving your cat proper basic care that you get to have a well behaved cat at home as a pet.

Chapter 7 - Care for Your Maine Coon

Living Quarters

Your cat's living quarters is its most important location. Although your cat obviously ventures into other rooms and in particular the living room, there are times when it will naturally retreat back to its living quarters. This is usually the time when it needs to catch a nap or simply relax. This makes it very important to know how to treat its living quarters.

Whether you have enough room at home and have designated a room for your cat or just created a special place in one of the rooms as your cat's living quarters, the room or space needs to be as clean as possible. You need to maintain cleanliness in the room or space as much as possible to make your cat feel comfortable. That cleanliness extends to ensuring that the litter box(s) and everything else in the room or space remains clean.

Just in the same way that you arrange your rooms in the best way possible, you need to ensure that your cat's living quarters is properly arranged. Do ensure that the litter box is far away from feeding/water dishes. The scratching post should also be strategically located for your cat to find it easy to perform its scratching ritual.

Grooming

"The only self-cleaning thing in this house is the cat". This is a very common phrase used on many refrigerator magnets and for good reason. By their nature, cats are the epitome of cleanliness and will go to great lengths to ensure that they remain clean at all times. This is why you observe your Maine Coon cat "licking" its face and other parts of the body with the tongue.

The "licking is not actual licking. It is actually a means through which your cat cleans itself, using the tongue as a washcloth. Cats generally have unique tongue; it is barbed, making it useful for a good number of purposes. It uses its tongue as grooming tool, using it to remove loose fur, in stripping away scent of food, in

Chapter 7 - Care for Your Maine Coon

---

getting rid of such parasites as flea, for increasing blood circulation and for controlling its body temperature. Your cat naturally applies saliva on its forepaw before embarking on the grooming routine.

The onset of self-grooming starts right when a cat is born. The mother naturally "licks" its kittens" to not only keep them clean but to also arouse them to suckle, to stimulate them to remove body waste (feces and urine) and to provide them with comfort, especially when it is hot. For the kittens, self-grooming starts when they are about four weeks old.

It is very important to know how your cat grooms itself to enable you to know how you will groom it. When self-grooming, your cat applies saliva to the inside part of one paw before cleaning itself in an upward circular pattern. It naturally starts by cleaning its nose before proceeding to the eyes, backside of the ears and eventually the forehead. Your cat does the same with the right paw. It is only after this that your cat embarks on grooming such other parts of the body as its front legs, shoulders, flanks, genital area, hind legs and the tail. This can be a time-consuming exercise, which can last for an hour.

The importance that cats in general attach to self-grooming makes it very necessary that you too come in to groom your cat. Indeed, the Maine Coon, just like other cat breeds do enjoy grooming. Grooming your cat does not only make it clean, doing so also goes a long way in developing a strong bond between you and your cat in addition to allowing you to screen for any visible skin problems.

One unique thing with the Maine Coon cat is that it does not shed heavily even though it is a long-haired cat. Even so, you need to frequently brush your cat to prevent development of hairballs, which in extreme cases require surgery to remove. Brushing your cat at least twice a week should be enough. You need to invest in

Chapter 7 - Care for Your Maine Coon

a quality de-shedding tool whose use requires gentle strokes so as to prevent pain. You also need to have a soft grooming brush to use alongside a de-shedding tool.

Removing mats from your cat's body is a very important part of grooming. Maine Coons are very prone to mats due to their long fur. It is therefore very necessary that you keep your cat on the safe side by removing mats in case you notice any. Mats can be extremely painful to a point where your cat will not be able to move. Although frequent brushing reduces the risk of mats, you need to invest in quality clippers just in case.

Ensuring that your cat's ears and eyes are clean through grooming is very important. You need to examine your cat's eyes and ears for any signs of debris that you need to clean out to prevent build up of the same. The ears are in particular prone to build up of wax that you need to remove frequently. You need to invest in an ear lobe and cotton balls that are effective in cleaning both the eyes and ears. You however need to be careful when cleaning your cat's ears. Restrict yourself to cleaning visible areas only.

Although your cat naturally indulges in its natural habit of scratching at the scratching post, you still need to examine its nails to ensure that they remain as short as possible. Make it a habit to trim your cat's nails only once in a month using a quality clipper. One area you need to avoid reaching when clipping is the triangular area of the paw that is usually pink in colour. Referred to as the quick, cutting into this area leads to bleeding, which can make it very difficult to clip your cat's nails next time since it will naturally develop fear.

It is important to note that you only need to clip the front paws. The hind paws rarely grow long. Unlike most cat breeds, the Maine Coon cat breed loves water. It is therefore appropriate to bathe your cat at least twice a week. It is during bathing that you can easily remove any mats that start developing. It is also during

Chapter 7 - Care for Your Maine Coon

bathing that you can effectively use your cat brush to smoothen and straighten its fur. You need to invest in quality medicated soap, shampoo and conditioning for bathing.

Grooming Products

There are a good number of cat grooming tools in the market that you need to invest in to make your cat clean, healthy and comfortable. These include brushes, flea/tick combs, sprays, shampoos, conditioners, clippers, scissors and lint removal tools. Some of the notable brands include Andis, Bio-Groom, Evercare and Oyster among other brands.

Although ignored by some cat owners, taking time to groom your Maine Coon cat is very important. You need to set apart at least an hour once in a week to groom your cat. This is particularly important considering that Maine Coons have long-fur and enjoy grooming.

Transportation

Cats and Maine Coon cats in particular make valuable pets. Not only are they adorable and make good companions; they also cheer you up when you are down in addition to making you remain active as you engage them in play. Unlike other cat breeds that are not fond of travelling, Maine Coons are very outgoing and love new environments. You however need to note that travelling with your cat in a car can make it very uncomfortable and most likely to vomit, pee and possibly get dehydrated, which can make your journey a very disappointing one.

You need to invest in a quality cat carrier in order to transport your cat without any problems. A carrier you buy should be spacious enough to allow your cat stand, turn around and stretch. It should also be very comfortable. The best way to transport your cat using a carrier is to have your cat get used to it several days before you travel. Because Maine Coons are generally large cats, you need to consider buying a bigger carrier.

Chapter 7 - Care for Your Maine Coon

As part of transport preparation, it is recommended that you consult with your vet for appropriate transport advice especially when you plan to travel with your cat over a long distance. Your vet will be able to prescribe medications and sprays that will calm your cat during the journey, in effect eliminating stress, which affects cats when being transported.

Food usually plays a major role in the comfort of a cat when travelling in a car. Your cat is most likely to vomit if you feed it just minutes before you embark on a journey. It is recommended that you feed your cat at least two hours before you set off to prevent vomiting. One serious mistake you need to avoid when travelling with your cat in a car is to let it out when you stop along the way. Your cat will become confused and possibly run away. Only let it out if you have a leash.

Exercises

Maine Coons are very good indoor and outdoor cats. Even so, you still need to subject your cat to different exercises. Depending on type of food, how frequently you feed it and the kind of treats you give it, your cat can easily gain excess body weight, which is a foundation for serious health conditions.
The only effective way to help your cat in maintaining a healthy body weight is through exercise. Exercising your cat is also beneficial even if it does not gain excess body weight. Exercising your cat goes a long way in ensuring that it remains physically fit.

By their nature, Maine Coons are generally very flexible animals and can perform different types of exercises. One of the simple exercises you may consider subjecting your cat to is by use of a laser pointer. Moving the laser around at different heights gives your cat a good opportunity to stretch as it moves to paw the light on a wall.

You definitely cannot ignore the importance of cat tree when it comes to exercising your cat. Having a cat tree gives your cat a

Chapter 7 - Care for Your Maine Coon

good opportunity to exercise as it climbs it. The other benefit of having a cat tree lies in the fact that you do not need to be around for your cat to exercise; it can do so even in your absence on its own. In absence of a cat tree, you need to ensure that there are no obstructions to windows to allow your cat jump on the windows as it pleases.

Having plenty of cat toys is beneficial to your cat in terms of exercise. Because of their playful nature, you need to have different types of cat toys that allow for different types of exercises. You may alternatively use readily available items at home instead of buying.

Many cat owners have of late found their treadmill valuable in exercising their cats and you too may consider the same if you happen to have one at home. Although your cat will learn quickly on how to walk and run on the mill, you will need to supervise it very closely.

One form of exercise you cannot ignore is taking your cat out for walks occasionally. A simple walk along the road or in a park exposes your cat to a new environment, which in itself provides for additional psychological benefits.

Cat Toys

Ensuring that your cat exercises on a regular basis is very important and there is no better way than to do so than with cat toys. Cat toys provide the opportunity for your cat to exercise both body and mind. Not only does your cat's body remain physically fit; its mental health is also enhanced in the process, relieving stress in addition to improving blood circulation within the body. Cat toys are also very effective in training a cat to abandon retrogressive behavior while at the same time acquiring progressive behavior.

There are basically four types of cat toys that you need to invest in:

Chapter 7 - Care for Your Maine Coon

Wand Toys

A wand toy does not need to be a special item. You can make use of a stick or a piece of cloth. Twitching (stick) or waving (cloth) in circles has the positive effect of enticing your cat. This is because such an item's movement becomes similar to a potential prey. You can add other enticing items on the wand to make it not only attractive but encouraging for your cat to keep on playing. Such other items you can add on the wand include coloured feathers.

It is very important that you keep the wand away from the cat once play session is over. Your cat should not get used to the wand because that may negate its usefulness during play. It will be similar to a cat getting used to a prey to a point that it does noting when the prey passes by. There are different wand brands in the market if you choose to buy.

Ball Toys

Balls are very effective as cat toys. Unlike ordinary balls however, cat ball toys are small. To your cat, the movement of these balls on the floor resembles scampering of potential prey, which entices your cat to a point that it chases after the balls. Like with a wand toy, a good way to effectively make use of cat balls is to add some niceties on the balls, niceties that your cat will strive to chase and grab. You have the option of buying ping-pong balls, sponge balls or Mylar balls among other balls.

Food-Dispensing Toys

These are the best toys to have when you plan to leave your cat at home for a long time in any given day. These toys literally deliver the food to your cat whenever it engages in play with them. One great benefit of these toys is that they teach your cat to work for its food, with the work being the play activity. This engages its mind, teaching it new tricks in the process. You can indeed make use of cat treats with these toys. Like with the other toys, there are

Chapter 7 - Care for Your Maine Coon

different brands of food-dispensing ball toys in the market you can choose from.

Catnip Toys
Catnip is a stimulating herb that cats really enjoy eating. Catnip toys are designed in such a way that they allow you to stuff catnip in them. The amount of catnip you stuff in is very critical because your cat can be over-stimulated.

Regardless of which cat toys you decide to buy, the toys should be those that stimulate your cat's natural instincts. The toys should mimic prey to encourage your cat to not only engage in play more but also master requisite intended techniques or behaviour.

Caring for a Pregnant Maine Coon Cat
Although you have the option of buying a spayed Maine Coon kitten/cat, you may also choose to buy one not subjected to the procedure, in which case it is bound to become pregnant when a partner is available or when you take it to a vet for that specific purpose. Caring for a pregnant Maine Coon, just like with caring for any pregnant cat differs greatly from caring for a non-pregnant cat in many respects.

From the onset, you need to know whether or not your cat has attained pregnancy. This should be at the earliest possible opportunity so that you adjust a number of things to suit its condition. Generally, a cat's gestation period ranges between 60 and 70 weeks and although you are not able to ascertain whether or not your cat is pregnant through urine or blood tests, there are specific signs you need to be on the lookout for.

The first sign of a cat's pregnancy is what is usually referred to as pinking up. This is the enlargement of a cat's nipples in which case the nipples not only become enlarged but become pinkish in colour as well. You are able to notice this when your cat is about three weeks pregnant.

Chapter 7 - Care for Your Maine Coon

Like in human females, pregnant cats gain weight naturally when pregnant. You will notice a gradual increase in body weight when you hold your cat and notice the pregnancy if you are keen. Increase in body weight usually occurs at the same time when pinking up occurs.

Another simple and clear sign of cat pregnancy that can help you know whether or not your cat is pregnant is morning sickness, just in the same way it happens to human females when they attain pregnancy. Clear sign of morning sickness in cats manifests in excessive sleep especially during morning hours and failure to eat or avoid certain food stuffs.

It is important that you take your cat to a vet for confirmation of pregnancy. A vet will be able to professionally ascertain your cat's pregnancy through palpitation. Even so, this will only be possible when the pregnancy is around four weeks. A vet may also opt to do an ultrasound but not X-ray in ascertaining pregnancy. With your cat's pregnancy confirmed, you need to quickly adjust several things. Your vet should indeed be in a position to inform you which adjustments you need to effect, one of which is nutrition. Your pregnant cat will need an increased amount of nutritious food. Amount of food should however not be excessive so as to prevent labour problems when the time comes for her to give birth.

This is also the time to ensure that your cat has access to safe drinking water at all times. You also need to allow your cat have as much rest as possible. She should only be engaged in play when she initiates the same. Your cat requires close monitoring during the whole period of pregnancy. Your vet will most likely advise you on when to take your cat for check-ups.

Apart from nutritious food, water and visits to the vet for check-ups, you need to buy several equipment and supplies in readiness for your cat giving birth. These include kitten box, surgical

Chapter 7 - Care for Your Maine Coon

gloves, syringe/eyedropper to aspirate nose/mouth secretions, cotton thread for ties, scissors, clean towels, antiseptic for cleaning umbilical and kitten milk replacer.

The last week of your cat's pregnancy is a very critical moment. This should find when you have introduced her to the kitten box, which you need to place in a quiet, warm location away from children. Because your cat is most likely to spend much time in her new location, you need to make food and water readily available.

There are a number of things you will notice when your cat will have gone into labour. First, her mammary glands will have increased tremendously in size. She will also most likely start nesting and have a general change in behaviour. Although you have made every effort to provide your cat with a kitten box, it can occur that your cat chooses to give birth elsewhere but within the house. This is perfectly normal and should not be a cause of concern. You will only need to transfer her and the kittens to the kitten box.

It is natural that your cat will give birth without your help. You however need to watch her very closely. There are several scenarios that will require that you call the vet since such may turn out to be emergency situations. These include excessive high body temperature, unpleasant smell of discharge, contractions lasting more than 20 minutes without any signs of kitten and protrusion of placenta through the vulva without any sign of kitten.

Taking care of the kitten should not be a big problem since your cat will do almost everything. You will however have specific responsibilities toward your cat. In addition to ensuring that you maintain high level of hygiene in your cat's room or space, you will need to ensure that your cat receives nutritious diet and supplements to properly feed the kitten. The kitten will be able to

Chapter 7 - Care for Your Maine Coon

start feeding on solid food when they are between four and five weeks, with introduction of solid food being on gradual basis.

It is only after six weeks that you can start weaning the kitten in readiness to selling them off or giving them off as gifts if you so wish. Maine Coons are very social animals and it is very necessary that you socialize the kittens as much as possible. Maine Coons develop very slowly and the period between six month and two years is particularly very important. This is the time the kittens need to be socialized, which can be by exposing them to your family members and letting them explore other spaces and rooms in the house.

One of the most important things you cannot ignore once your cat gives birth is the need to have the kittens wormed and vaccinated. Your vet should be in a good position to advise you on when this should be done. It is important to point out that although your cat can take up to between eight and ten weeks to become pregnant again, the possibility that she can attain another pregnancy at two weeks after giving birth remains high. This is one of the reasons why many cat owners choose to have their female cats spayed. You will therefore need to take precautions to prevent your cat falling pregnant again soon after giving birth, unless you intend it to be so.

One serious challenge you may face once your cat gives birth is when your cat rejects her kittens. This can be very challenging since you will have the responsibility of hand raising the kittens. Generally, Maine Coons give birth to few kittens, in most cases between two and three kittens. It should however not surprise you to find out that your cat has given birth to up to four kittens.

Chapter 8 – Feeding

Nutrition

Your cat requires appropriate nutrients necessary for body development, growth and general function of the body. These nutrients reside in the food that you feed your cat on. Failure to feed your cat on nutritious food stuffs definitely leads to specific nutrient-deficiency illnesses/diseases, some that are obviously life-threatening. Maine Coons in particular need very nutritious foods owing to their huge body and muscular nature.

Just in the same way that you pay close attention to what you eat, you also need to pay close attention to what you feed your cat on and in particular when it comes to food composition, which informs nutrition value of the food.

Of all nutrients, water is probably the most important nutrient that your cat needs, although it cannot survive on water alone. The fact that a big percentage of your cat's body weight is literally made up of water makes it very necessary that you supply your cat with fresh drinking water on a daily basis. Lack of water in the body does not only interfere with smooth metabolism; it can also be a cause of serious illnesses.

Your cat also needs sufficient amount of protein. Protein plays a very important role in the body and in particular in the formation of body cells, tissues, enzymes, organs, antibodies, enzymes and hormones. Your cat's body also requires protein for repair of body tissues and proper maintenance of the body.

Closely related to protein are amino acids that your cat also requires. Amino acids are literally the building blocks of proteins and while your cat's body can easily synthesize non-essential amino acids from its diet, its body cannot naturally synthesize

Chapter 8 - Feeding

such essential amino acid as taurine, which makes it necessary for your cat's food to contain the same.

Your cat does not only require water and protein. It also requires fats. Fats are very important when it comes to production of specific hormones and in cell structure. Fats are also required by the body for proper utilization of certain vitamins. The food you feed your cat on must contain such essential fats as linoleic and arachidonic acids. Lack of these fats can easily lead to your cat suffering from reduced growth and skin problems.

As has already been indicated elsewhere, Maine Coons are very playful and therefore require a lot of energy to remain active. This is why you need to feed your Maine Coon cat on carbohydrates. Carbohydrates do not only provide your cat's body with the energy it requires; carbohydrates play a critical role in maintaining good health of the intestine. You however need to note that cats are generally carnivorous animals and therefore need very little amount of carbohydrates.

Vitamins are the other very important nutrients that your cat needs. Different vitamins play different roles in the body with some vitamins required for enzyme reaction. Since your cat's body cannot synthesize most vitamins, it is very necessary that the food you feed your cat on contains all the required vitamins. Like with the other nutrients, lack of vitamins leads to occurrence of various vitamin-deficiency illnesses.

Lastly, your cat requires sufficient supply of minerals for proper bone and teeth development, for metabolic processes and for maintenance of appropriate fluid balance within the body. Because your cat's body cannot synthesize minerals, you must ensure that your cat food contains these vital inorganic compounds.

Although your cat definitely needs different nutrients to grow and remain healthy, the amount of nutrients you feed your cat is very

Chapter 8 - Feeding

critical. This is so because cats require different amounts of nutrients depending on their age.

Kitten Nutrition Needs

You definitely have no role to play when it comes to feeding kitten with nutrients. Kittens obtain all the nutrients they need for their first few weeks from their mother's milk, which contains all the necessary nutrients. There are instances where kitten mother may not be around because of death, illness or when the mother rejects her kitten upon giving birth. In such instance, formulated commercial milk is always the best option.

Unlike other cat breed kittens, Maine Coon kittens grow very slowly. The commercial milk you buy must therefore contain adequate amounts of all the nutrients in balanced quantities. It is important to point out that kittens do require energy three times that of adult cats and proteins two times that of adults.

Adult Cat Nutrition Needs

Meeting nutrition needs of an adult cat can be a serious challenge. Not only should an adult cat have enough to eat but also consume a diet rich in all the necessary nutrients. An adult Maine Coon cat is not only active and therefore requires increased amount of energy; it also requires increased amount of protein for repair of body tissues and for other body functions as well. It also requires increased amount of essential fats particularly during cold weather. Although it is very necessary that you feed your cat on these, you need to be careful so as not to make your cat obese.

It is very important to note that although your adult cat will need the same amount of nutrients during adulthood, there are exceptions. Periods when your cat is sick or pregnant will definitely raise the need to buy food containing nutrients necessary taking into account your cat's condition.

Chapter 8 - Feeding

Old Cat Nutrition Needs
Just in the same way that feeding kittens and adult cats differ, feeding an old cat also differs. You are most likely to start noticing your Maine Coon cat's aging signs when it is about fifteen years. Because of body composition, metabolic and immunologic changes it is bound to go through, occurrence of such age-related diseases/health conditions as loss of muscle mass, arthritis, obesity and dental problems among others become common.

Taking into account the changes in an old cat's body and the likelihood of development of the indicated diseases/health conditions, a diet for an old cat should be one that promotes good health and appropriate body weight. Such a diet should ideally be low on carbohydrates but high on proteins, vitamins, essential fatty acids and minerals.

The Right Food
You have two options when it comes to the right food for your cat; canned and dry food, which at times is referred to as dry kibble. Compared with canned food, dry food stuffs have low water content, high on carbohydrates and plant protein. Considering that cats are carnivorous animals, dry kibble is not the right food for your cat.

Although your cat needs foods rich in protein, it is better off with animal-based protein. Feeding your cat plant-based protein derived from vegetables simply has no value to your cat in terms of nutrition. Unlike plant-based protein, animal-based protein contains amino acids, the essential fats that are beneficial to your cat. Canned food contains animal-based protein, making canned food the right food for your cat.

Although canned food cannot be said to be that fresh, dry kibble goes through a lot of processing in addition to being cooked at high temperatures for long times. This does not only lower quality of protein within but also damages other nutrients.

Chapter 8 - Feeding

The benefit of canned cat food over dry kibble is also in the amount of water contained. Cats generally do not drink water since their prey in the wild supplies them with enough amount of water. Having a cat at home therefore requires that you feed it on a diet rich in water, which makes canned food the right food for your cat.

You have two options when it comes to cat food. The first option is to prepare cat food on your own at home or buy commercial canned foods. It is important to look at these two options to enable you make the right decision when it comes to food for your cat.

Unknown to some cat owners, cats are carnivorous animals and therefore rely on eating raw meat. Whether it is fresh or raw meat is neither here nor there since wild cats kill their prey and may not consume the whole prey in one instance. Cat owners who have a negative view on feeding their cats on raw meat therefore deny their cats what they are actually supposed to eat. A common belief by such cat owners usually has to do with the element of food poisoning.

Unlike us humans who are highly susceptible to food poisoning, cats are not. This is because while the food we eat resides in our intestines for anything between 35 and 55 hours, the food that a cat eats only resides in its intestine for between 12 and 16 hours. This simply means that any harmful bacteria remain within a cat's intestine for a short period of time unlike in humans. The short period of time therefore lowers the risk of food poisoning.

It is therefore perfectly in order to buy raw meat to feed your cat on. Even as you do so, you need to remember that not all raw meat sources are the same in quality. You need to consider buying whole cuts of meat that you can thoroughly clean before feeding your cat on instead of buying pre-ground meats available in supermarkets.

Chapter 8 - Feeding

It can be very fulfilling if you opt to prepare for your cat its food at home. Even as you do so, it is very important that you do not subject your cat to the same meat source. You seriously need to consider changing meat sources. You have the option of feeding your cat on beef, rabbit meat or chicken among others. You also need to consider adding in some water and recommended supplements.

The second option is to go for commercial cat food and in this case canned cat foods. There is however a serious challenge you are likely to face when shopping for canned cat food; marketing gimmicks or food labels. Some of the food labels you are most likely to come across on canned cat foods include "For Indoor-Only Cat", "Natural", "Premium", "Breed Specific", Veterinarian Recommended" and "Therapeutic Diet" among other labels.

Although they seem very promising, some of the food labels can be very misleading. The reality is that most canned foods with these labels contain wheat, corn, soy and by-products. While wheat, corn and soy definitely have high levels of carbohydrate that your cat does not really need, the by-products happen to be the only source of protein for your cat, which is not appropriate.

The only effective way to overcome the challenge presented by promising yet false food labels is to look at both the composition and ingredients used in making canned cat food when shopping. While the composition part of it refers to percentage of fat, protein and carbohydrate cat food contains, ingredients refer to the specific nutrients in the food. You need to pay attention to three important things when it comes to choosing the right canned cat food; it should food be food that is high in water content, low in carbohydrates and contain animal-based protein instead of plant-based protein.

It is worth pointing out that mainstream canned cat foods can at times be very expensive, depending on your location. This is because they do contain muscle meat of chicken and turkey among others, which is normally listed as the first ingredient. Depending on your financial position, you may consider buying canned cat foods that contain by-products. These are normally labeled as "chicken by-products" or "turkey by-products" among others. The fact that they are affordable does not mean that they are of no nutrition value.

Like with all canned foods, canned cat foods do feature preservatives and ascertaining the kind of preservative used in cat food is very important. There are canned cat foods that contain such preservatives as ethoxyguin, BHA and BHT. These are chemicals that have been proved not to be safe when used as preservatives. Although most cat food manufacturers have abandoned the use of such preservatives, you need to check to ensure that canned cat food you are about to buy does not contain the same.

Feeding Program
There is really no uniform cat feeding program. This is the frequency at which you need to feed your cat. How frequently you feed your Maine Coon kitten, adult cat or an old cat definitely differs. This is because they need to feed at different intervals and in different amounts at every stage of their life. Your home environment and type of food you feed your cat on also informs feeding frequency.

Just like with human babies, kittens need to be fed small amounts of food at regular intervals. This is because their tummies are not yet capable of handling large amounts of food yet this is the time they need sufficient amount of various nutrients necessary for growth and development. Maine Coon kittens generally need to be fed at least four meals spread out in any given day.

Unlike kittens that need to eat nutritious food for growth and development, your adult Maine Coon cat needs to eat maintenance food. This is food that does not only aid in further development of the body but in maintaining strong healthy bones

Chapter 8 - Feeding

and in enhancing the body's immune system. Because it can be difficult to ascertain the amount of food that your adult cat needs, it is better to let it eat until it is satisfied. Two meals in any given day should be enough.

Just in the same way that feeding kittens differs from feeding adult cats, feeding an old Maine Coon cat also differs. Old cats are generally susceptible to various diseases and health conditions that make it necessary to tailor their feeding frequency taking into account any health problems they may have. The same goes for sick kittens and adult cats.

It is important to look at the feeding program for adult cats because such is the cat you are most likely to have. You have two options when it comes to designing a feeding program for your cat. Your first option is to let your cat get used to free feeding program where you fill its feeding dish with large amount of food that it can eat when it wishes. Although this program best suits a cat that is often left alone at home for a considerable amount of time, it has its disadvantages. First, you are obligated to buy kibble cat food because fresh food may not last long in the open. Secondly, there is the risk of your cat over-eating and therefore developing obesity.

Your other option is to design a scheduled feeding program where your cat gets used to a specific time when it is served food. This program can be very beneficial considering the fact that you are literally in a position to control how much food your cat consumes at any given time.

The fact that you have designed a feeding program for your cat should not mean that such a program is permanent. There is always room to alter a program depending on different situations such as when travelling, when your cat is sick, when your cat is pregnant (if a female and not spayed) and when adverse weather changes occur.

Chapter 8 - Feeding

Food Allergies

Just like it is with humans, cats too develop different allergies including inhalant, flea bite and food allergies. In the case of food, cats generally develop food allergy when subjected to specific food stuff on a regular basis. Maine Coons do develop allergies when they are between two and six years although a few have been noted to develop food allergy as early as when they are five months old and when they are as old ad fifteen years old.

Contrary to a popular belief, food allergy does not necessarily mean food intolerance. Unlike food intolerance that manifests itself in form of diarrhoea and/or vomiting, food allergy exhibits real symptoms that may include itchy skin, hair loss and excessive scratching among other symptoms.

Causes of food allergy in cats are usually specific ingredients found in cat foods and in particular in such cat food stuffs as corn, soy, dairy products, wheat and seafood. It is worth noting that these are the same food stuffs found in dry or kibble cat foods.

Determining whether or not your cat suffers from food allergy can be a very big challenge. This is because food allergy symptoms are in most cases similar to those presented by such cat diseases/health conditions as flea bite allergy and intestinal parasite hypersensitivity. There are however several ways through which you can determine whether or not your cat suffers from food allergy or other disease, although determination can take some time.

The most effective way through which you can determine whether or not your cat suffers from food allergy is to undertake food trial. This means subjecting your cat to a specific type of food for several days while looking out for any allergy symptoms. It is important to note that blood tests are only effective in diagnosing other types of allergies but not food allergy.

Chapter 8 - Feeding

There are instances where your cat's food allergy and associated symptoms become serious. This is usually the time to take your cat to a vet for examination and treatment. Your vet will most likely feed your cat fatty acids, steroids and prescribe antihistamines as the first line of treatment. The only effective way of treating food allergy in cats is avoidance of causative food.

What Not to Feed Your Cat

Food that is edible to you and/or your dog may not be edible to your cat. Feeding your cat on certain food stuffs cannot only cause allergies and intoxication, consumption of certain food stuffs can easily lead to your cat going into coma with increased risk of instant death.

It is perfectly normal to have alcoholic beverages at home so long as you keep them safe and away from your cat. Your cat will definitely be intoxicated when it consumes any food containing alcohol and can easily go into coma with high chances of dying.

Spices make food very tasty but only for humans. Feeding your cat on spices can cause serious allergic reaction and toxicity, which can lead to death.

Cats are carnivorous animals and therefore do well with meat but not bones. Whether from fish, beef, lamb or poultry, bones are simply dangerous to your cat. Not only can they cause obstruction; bones can also lacerate your cat's digestive system and cause serious problems.

You should not feed or let your cat feed on such food stuffs as tea, chocolate, coffee and caffeine. These contain caffeine, theophylline and theobromine. These are ingredients that cause vomiting and other health problems in cats.

While both human vitamin and mineral supplements can indeed be healthy, they can be very dangerous when you feed your cat on

Chapter 8 - Feeding

them. You need to keep all your food supplements far from reach of your cat.

These are just a few of food stuffs that you should not feed your cat on. Although your cat will naturally avoid some of these food stuffs, you need to safely keep away those that it can accidentally consume.

Cat Treats

Giving your cat treats occasionally is highly recommended. Contrary to common belief by some cat owners, cat treats are not entirely valueless. Modern cat treats are formulated to encourage good dental, digestive, general and skin health, depending on type of treat you buy. Note that there are crunchy, dental, soft, catnip/grass and jerky cat treats. You also have the option of buying grain-free, natural or organic cat treats. To enhance their appeal and taste, cat treats are in most cases flavoured. You may choose to buy beef, chicken, vegetarian, turkey, tuna or fish flavoured treats. Your cat definitely needs intake of calories that cat treats provide. However, it is very important that you measure the amount of treats you feed your cat on. Because cat treats largely contain calories, they should not make up more than 10% of your cat's calorie intake. Your cat should obtain the remaining 90% from quality nutritious foods.

Like with shopping for canned cat food, it is important that you choose cat treats with utmost care. This is because some information contained on cat treat labels may not be correct. You seriously need to look out for amount of calories a cat treat food contains before you buy.

When to feed your cat treats is very important. This is because there is increased risk of your cat developing addiction or taste for treats instead of its regular foods. Because of this, you need to feed your cat treats at special occasions only. Such can be when it does something positive like mastering a rule and excelling in an

Chapter 8 - Feeding

exercise or training. Because cat treats basically contain calories, they are not recommended for overweight cats. Feeding your overweight cat treats will simply worsen its condition and increase the risk of serious health conditions. For an overweight cat, go for Catnip/grass treats. Both are cereal grasses and therefore low on calories.

You should be able to find different types of cat treats in the market. There are those that are soft and moist and those that are hard, just similar to dry cat food. You cat will most likely hate dry treats in favour of soft treats. It is always a good idea to balance between the two for your cat to receive all the nutrients it needs for good health.

There are a number of cat treat brands in the market and just like with choosing canned food carefully, you need to choose cat treats carefully. The most important things to look into are the ingredients a treat is composed of. This is very necessary because some cat treats may contain ingredients that may cause allergies. How you store cat treats you buy is of great importance. The Maine Coon is a very clever cat and will notice when you feed it on treats. It will therefore look for the same where you store its canned food. It may develop the habit of stealing treats if you fail to store the same in a secure place. The best way to go about storing cat treats is to store the same in a different location from where you store its regular food.

Chapter 9 – Training

Cat Training

Cat training refers to the practice of instilling certain values in your cat. It is a wide area that also involves changing some of your cat's natural but unpleasant behaviour. Cat training provides for several benefits not only to you but to your cat as well. A well trained cat usually has its body and mind well stimulated, which goes a long way in enhancing its overall health. Well trained cats also exhibit good behaviour especially in the presence of visitors. It is also through training that you build a close relationship with your cat. Failure to give your cat the necessary training can easily turn your cat into a pest instead of a pet.

Cat training requires that you first understand your cat in different respects. Luckily, Maine Coons are not only highly intelligent buts also very easy to train and remain obedient. You can easily train your Maine Coon cat to stop doing something or to behave in a certain manner at certain times. Like other animals, cats do learn through experience. Your cat will stop doing something from which it has a bad experience with.

You have two options when it comes to training your cat. You have the option of taking your cat to a dedicated cat or pet training centre, invite a cat or pet trainer to your home or undertake the training on your own. Because taking your cat somewhere else or engaging the service of a trainer involves expenses, you may consider undertaking the training on your own. Training your cat personally can be very fulfilling especially when you see your cat positively responding to your instructions.

Chapter 9 - Training

One thing you must avoid at all costs when training your cat is punishment. Unlike dogs, cats respond negatively to reprimands and punishments. Punishing or reprimanding your cat for failing to follow given instruction develops fear in your cat, which makes training very difficult. Furthermore, a fearful cat will always try to run away. The secret to training your cat effectively lies in using treats. Rewarding your cat with treats whenever it does something positive or when it responds positively and follows given instructions is the only sure way through which you can give your cat proper training. There are three basic areas where you need to train your cat; house training, behavioural training and trick training.

House Training

You share almost every room in your home with your cat. Although it tends to spend most of its time in its room/space or outdoors, it will on a regular basis venture into the other rooms for companionship or to simply explore the other rooms. This makes it necessary to train it properly in different areas.

Litter training is the most important house training that you must give your cat. You must however ensure that the litter box is not only clean at all times but placed in the most appropriate location within the cat's room or space. One reason why cats do avoid their litter box and instead choose to urinate or go for long call in other places in the house is usually due to dirty litter. Note that what may seem clean to you may not necessarily be clean to a cat. You need to get accustomed to changing the litter on a daily basis before you can embark on litter training.

You need to start introducing your cat to its litter box immediately you bring it home. Although filling the litter box with dry and clean soil will naturally attract the cat when it needs to pee or go for long call, you still need to introduce your cat to it. It is highly recommended that you place the litter box away from the cat's sleeping quarters and feeding/water dishes. Apart from

Chapter 9 - Training

litter box training, you need to train your cat on where to sit or lie when in the living room.

Behavioural Training

Behavioural training is probably the most extensive and difficult part of cat training. This is because of the many behavioural changes you need to train your cat to adopt or discard.

Your cat naturally has a hunting instinct and will naturally bite or claw your hands when you engage it in play activities. Although this is normal cat behaviour, you need to train your Maine Coon cat to abandon this behaviour. The best way to offer the training is during play sessions where you stop play immediately when it bites or claws. This is also the best time to use treats, denying your cat the same when it engages in biting and clawing.

Your action of stopping to play and denying it treats sends a strong message to the cat that it is out of its behaviour that play has not only stopped but it has been denied treats as well. You are most likely to notice change in this behaviour during play sessions that follow when your cat resorts to using its paws instead of teeth and nails during play. This is also the time to effectively make use of treats, rewarding it for not biting and clawing.

Cats do communicate by meowing. Your cat will naturally meow when hungry, when in danger, when in need of a mate (in case of non-spayed female cat), to attract your attention or when requesting something. Although perfectly normal, excessive meowing can be a serious problem in the house. Your first reaction to your cat's excessive meowing should be to consult your vet with the aim of ascertaining whether or not your cat suffers from an illness or disease.

It is also important to note that such changes in the house as re-arranging the house can make a cat meow a lot. It is equally

Chapter 9 - Training

important to note that you may be the cause of excessive meowing if you have made your cat develop the habit of meowing by giving it something whenever it meows. The most effective way to train your cat to stop excessive meows is to give something like a treat when it is quiet and denying it the same when it meows.

While having a playful Maine Coon cat as a pet is perfectly in order, in can be a big challenge when you have a hyperactive and playful Maine Coot cat. Your hyperactive cat will indulge in such activities as too much play, hiding things in the house, chasing unseen mice, jumping on and off furniture and in extreme cases stealing.

Cats that do exhibit this behaviour are in most cases hyperactive cats not engaged in play activities and often left alone. The most effective way to get your cat to abandon such behaviour is to provide means such as play activities through which your cat can expend the excess energy. In case of an un-spayed or un-neutered cat, this may also be the right time to have it neutered/spayed.

One of the most misunderstood cat behaviour by many cat owners is cat's territorial behaviour. Like such other wild cats as Leopards, your Maine Coon cat will naturally mark its territory within the house, which can be every room and items in the house including furniture. Note that cats have a high sense of smell and will detect any foreign smell however light the same may be.

Your cat has scent glands located along its tail, on its front paws, either side of its forehead, on its chin and its lips. Its behaviour of rubbing its tail or head on you or anything else in the house is therefore not a way of grooming itself but as a way of marking its territory by picking up smell and leaving its smell on the same.

Although it is natural for your cat to mark its territory, the same can be on the extreme. Note that cats engage in this behaviour as

Chapter 9 - Training

one way of guarding themselves from possible threats. The scent they leave behind when marking their territory is meant to serve as a warning to other cats that the area is already occupied. The only effective way to train your cat to abandon this behaviour that at times can be irritating is to socialize with your cat as much as possible. Your cat should never feel threatened in any way.

Having an untrained cat at home as a pet can be very dangerous in a case where you also have a bird or birds as pets. By their nature, cats have hunting and chasing instinct. Although your cat may not chase after prey which in such a case is the bird to kill for food, it will chase out of instinct with the aim of tossing the bird around, which can result in serious injuries to the bird. This is predatory behaviour that is very common with both indoor and outdoor cats including Maine Coon cats.

Persistent predatory behaviour stems from the fact that your cat will not have opportunity to vent out its natural instinct and therefore directs the same to the potential in-house pet. The only effective way to offer predatory training is to have your cat socialize with a potential prey under close watch. Such socialization makes the cat realize that the potential prey is indeed part of the family.

Nocturnal Training
Your Maine Coon cat is naturally a nocturnal animal. It will spend a lot of time sleeping during the day and become active during the night when you are deep asleep. Its night activities can be very disturbing if you do not offer appropriate training. Your cat will naturally become active from late in the evening to early morning.

Letting your cat get used to this schedule will deny you quality sleep. The most appropriate training you offer should aim at changing its schedule of activities, which you can do by engaging it in play activities during the day instead of letting it sleep.

Chapter 9 - Training

Because changing its schedule can be challenging, you need to go about doing so gradually until it gets used to the new schedule.

Even so, you will still not stop your cat from engaging in night activities albeit to a smaller degree. You therefore still need to make suitable cat play toys available to allow your cat engage in some activities during the night. You however need to set up the toys away from your bedroom to avoid sleep disruption.

Trick Training

One reason why Maine Coons make good companions is the fact that they are receptive to trick training. You can train your Maine Coon cat to do a number of things in the house including ringing the door bell or playing dead.

Dominance Training

Maine Coon's figure is itself very dominating. It is naturally independent and can easily defend itself against attacks by other cats. However, there are times when dominance training becomes necessary. It is through dominance training that your cat gains the confidence it needs when in the presence of other cats. This training is particularly useful in case you live in an area with many other cats in the neighbourhood and your cat ventures out a lot.

Command Training

This is one of the most important trainings you have to subject your cat to. Your cat should be able to positively respond to such commands as come, roll, go and sit. This training requires a lot of time and patience on your part because your cat will obviously not master all the commands you give in one training session.

Leash Training

Walking on a leash is the other important training you must offer your cat. This is so because you will occasionally take your cat out for walks. Unlike most cat breeds however, Maine Coon

Chapter 9 - Training

breed is very receptive to walking on a leash. Even so, it is highly recommended that you place the leash near its food dish or other favourite location where it sees it often to get used to it. It pays to only buy a harness specially designed for cats. Such do have the leash attachment located behind the harness and not at the neck.

Training Rules

- Regardless of type of training, be patient but committed to your cat's training schedule.
- Never resort to punishing your cat in case it fails to perform as expected. Punishing it will make it develop fear and therefore fail to master any training that you offer.
- It pays to embark on training at a slow pace, training a single item for several days before introducing another item.
- Always reward your cat whenever it performs better for encouragement.
- Set a specific training time everyday. This will get your cat accustomed to training routine

Chapter 10 – Health

Maine Coon Cat Health

Although people-oriented, lovely and very appealing, the Maine Coon cat breed is one breed susceptible to several diseases/health conditions. However, this is not to say that other cats are not susceptible to the same diseases/health conditions that Maine Coon cats are susceptible to. Most of Maine Coon cat diseases/health conditions can easily be prevented through proper recommended feeding and regular veterinary care. Most of the diseases/health conditions happen to be hereditary.

Common Illnesses/Diseases

Hypertrophic Cardiomyopathy (HCM)

This is the most serious hereditary disease that Maine Coon cats do suffer from. However, all other cats remain susceptible to the disease. The disease causes stiffening of the heart wall, in effect restricting flow of blood. This can lead to instant heart failure. Although the disease presents no symptoms, such symptoms as lethargy, excessive weight loss, labored breathing, excessive heart murmur and lameness on rear legs should be a cause of concern.

It is important that you take your cat to a vet immediately when you notice any of these symptoms for proper check up, diagnosis and treatment.

Chapter 10 - Health

Spinal Muscular Atrophy (SMA)

This is another hereditary disease that Maine Coon cats remain susceptible to. It affects kittens in most cases. While an affected kitten remains normal in other areas of the body, the rear legs show signs of lameness. This is because the disease impairs neurons found within the spinal cord.

Reputable Maine cat breeders to engage vets to carry out tests on their kittens to ascertain presence of the disease before the kittens are sold off.

Kidney Disease

Kidney disease is one disease that is often ignored when looking at cat diseases. All cats regardless of breed are susceptible to kidney disease. The kidney plays the important role of removing waste from the bloodstream in addition to regulating amount of fluids in the body. Failure by the kidneys to play these vital roles puts a cat's life in serious danger.

Kidney disease presents different symptoms including loss of appetite, frequent vomiting, depression, poor coat appearance and frequent urination or no urination. Kidney disease can be acute or sudden and chronic or long-term. It can be caused by such factors as trauma, surgery, shock, serious blood loss, poison, drugs and infection of the kidneys.

Unlike other cat diseases that present symptoms almost immediately, symptoms associated with kidney disease only appear when a large part of the kidneys is already destroyed. It is therefore very necessary that you take your cat for regular veterinary check ups.

Chapter 10 - Health

Hip Dysplasia

Maine Coon cats are highly susceptible to Hip Dysplasia largely because of the huge size. This is a hereditary disease that affects joints of the hip, in effect making it impossible for the cat's legs to support its weight. When left untreated for a long time, the disease can cause disintegration of cartilage, leading to arthritis.

While these are the diseases that Maine Coon cats remain highly susceptible to, they are also at risk of suffering from other diseases/health conditions that affect other cat breeds. These include:

Gingivitis

Gingivitis is a periodontal disease. It causes inflammation of the gums that turn reddish. Plaque formation also occurs. Plaque is basically a collection of debris, food, dead skin, mucous and bacteria. The gingival surface however remains very smooth. The disease can easily be reversed at the earliest stage through proper dental care.

Without proper dental care, the disease develops further with occurrence of calculus under the gums. Calculus is a mixture of organic matter, carbonate and calcium phosphate. In addition to further development of plaque, the gum surface becomes irregular with some pain in the gums.

As the disease progresses, it forms a narrow space between the teeth and the inner wall of the gum. The bacteria present in this space mutate and release toxins that damage gingival tissue. Occurrence of gingivitis is common not only in cats but also in dogs aged three years and above.

Apart from the swelling and reddishness of the gums, other symptoms of the disease include bad breath. Gingivitis is largely caused by accumulation of plaque. There are also other risk factors that encourage occurrence of the disease. These include excessive soft food, old age, bad chewing habits, diabetes, breathing through the mouth, crowded teeth and autoimmune disease among other risk factors.

Because of the danger that gingivitis poses to your cat, you need to help your cat in preventing occurrence of the disease. This you can do by ensuring that your cat's oral health remains at its optimum by brushing its teeth at least twice in a week with veterinarian toothpaste or using a finger pad to clean the teeth. This simple action goes a long way in preventing build-up of plaque.

A serious case of gingivitis requires veterinarian attention at the earliest possible time. In addition to physical examination, your vet will, as a matter of routine, try to establish possible causes of the disease, which can be the kind of food you feed your cat on.

There are several ways through which your vet may choose to treat the disease, depending on his/her findings. Your vet may prescribe antibacterial solution for squirting on your cat's teeth to prevent build-up of plaque, prescribe dietary supplements or prescribe specific foods that help in promoting good dental health.

In case of serious gingivitis, your vet may choose to remove baby (deciduous) teeth that may cause teeth overcrowding, which is a cause of the disease or remove particular affected teeth. It is also possible that your vet may choose to only remove plaque and calculus before polishing teeth surface.

Gingivitis is a serious gum disease that you must not let your cat suffer from. This is so because it reaches a stage where your cat will not be able to chew food properly or even eat due to pain. You will certainly not rule out malnourishment and possible death of your pet.

Chapter 10 - Health

Familial Amyloidosis

This is not a disease but rather a health condition that affects the liver. It is actually a group of disorders with similar characteristic; abnormal deposition of Amyloid (a fibrous protein) into body tissues. Amyloid occurs as a hard and waxy substance and develops as a result of degeneration of tissue. The disposition interferes with the normal functioning of areas where the protein has reached. Familial Amyloidosis is a hereditary health disorder common in Abyssinian, Burmese and Siamese breed of cats although it can also affect Maine Coons.

Although this is a hereditary disorder, it can also be caused by various factors including chronic infection, inflammation of inner layer of the heart caused by bacterial endocarditis and tumour. The condition presents several symptoms including general body weakness, loss of appetite, excessive thirst and urination, vomiting, enlarged abdomen and swelling of the limbs accompanied by joint pain.

Familial Amyloidosis is not treatable. It is a disorder that impairs the liver, seriously affecting its function and that of other body organs and most cats die from the disease. There are however specific measures that your vet can take to lessen the pain and help prolong your cat's life in case of infection. Your vet may take such measures as blood transfusion (blood change), fluid therapy, diet change and in some cases surgery.

Retinol Atrophy

Retinal atrophy is a non-treatable hereditary disease common in some cat breeds. The disease is also common in some dog breeds. It is the degeneration of retina, causing gradual loss of vision, which ends in blindness. The disease presents such symptoms as decreased vision at night, dilated pupils and cataract formation among other symptoms.

Chapter 10 - Health

Hyperthyroidism

This is an endocrine disorder whose occurrence is directly linked to over-activity of the thyroid gland, which leads to excess levels of specific hormones. These hormones play a very important role in the body; the role of controlling metabolism. Increased levels of these hormones have the negative effect of increasing your cat's heart rate with the possibility of your cat developing heart murmur. Without appropriate treatment, the disease easily causes heart failure, kidney damage, high blood pressure and death.

Your cat will exhibit a number of symptoms when infected. These include diarrhoea, vomiting, behavioural changes, weight loss, increased thirst and urination, body weakness, poor coat condition and rapid heartbeat among other symptoms. These symptoms may not necessarily point at hyperthyroidism because the same symptoms are presented by other cat diseases including cat diabetes and renal failure. It is therefore very important that you take your cat to a vet once you notice any of these symptoms.

The fact that hyperthyroidism does not affect specific breeds of cats means that all cats are at risk of suffering from the disease. It mostly affects older cats and dogs. There are two main ways of treating hyperthyroidism. A treatment method a vet chooses depends on your cat's medical condition.

Your vet may choose to prescribe such medications as Tapazole whose action is not to treat but to control the disease. Your cat will however need to use prescribed medication(s) for the rest of its life. There are instances when a vet may choose to undertake surgery with the aim of removing enlarged thyroid. The other treatment your vet may choose is to implement radioactive iodine treatment, which involves injection of a single dose of radioactive iodine. Iodine has the positive effect of destroying the damaged part of the thyroid while leaving normal thyroid tissues intact.

Chapter 10 - Health

Pyruvate Kinase Deficiency

Pyruvate Kinase is an enzyme whose deficiency in your cat's body leads to impairment of red blood cells, greatly reducing the ability of red blood cells to metabolize. The inability of red blood cells to metabolize causes anaemia in addition to other blood issues. Pyruvate Kinase deficiency is very common in such breed of cats as the Somali, Maine Coon, Abyssinian and other short-haired cat breeds including the Ocicat.

Caused by defects in genes acquired at birth, Pyruvate Kinase deficiency presents such symptoms as body weakness, anaemia, jaundice and increased heart rate among other symptoms. This condition is usually addressed through bone marrow transplant, which is the only treatment method available. In addition to being an expensive treatment, it is also life-threatening. Most cats that suffer from this condition die by the time they attain four years.

Arthritis

Arthritis refers to negative changes that occur within joints. These changes develop when cartilage that protects different bone joints wear out, causing friction at the joints. The friction causes swelling accompanied by pain. Although the cartilage is supposed to be replaced naturally, arthritis is bound to occur when it wears out faster than it is replaced.

Just like in humans, onset of arthritis in cats is in advanced age although middle aged cats can also suffer from the condition. The swelling and accompanying pain is usually chronic, which causes a lot of discomfort.

There is no cure for Arthritis. It can only be treated with any treatment that a vet offers, treatment that aims at lessening the pain and swelling that your cat experiences. Treatment needs to

Chapter 10 - Health

be offered at the earliest possible time so as to prevent further loss of cartilage.

Although arthritis is common in such other cat breeds as the Himalayan, Siamese and Persian cat breeds, your Maine Coon cat can suffer from the condition due to such factors as old age, obesity, congenital defects, accidents and infection.

Arthritis has a serious effect on a cat's health. This is because it does not only make a cat uncomfortable but impairs its mobility as well. The condition presents such symptoms as limited activity, stiffness in walking, limping and social withdrawal.

Although your vet will definitely prescribe medications that help in preventing swelling and managing pain, he/she is likely to recommend the most appropriate diet for your cat as the most effective treatment option. This is because food plays a very important role in your cat's overall health.

Allergic Dermatitis

Allergic dermatitis refers to conditions that affect the skin negatively. These can be caused by such factors as food allergy, parasites, hormonal imbalances and infections. One effective way to prevent allergic dermatitis in your cat is to feed it on food rich in meat-based protein, essential fatty acids and antioxidants. There are however instances when you may need to take your cat to a vet. This is when the skin is not only rough but has wounds. Your cat's skin should be smooth and soft without any signs of flakes. Hair on the skin should also be evenly spread out.

Diabetes

Just like in humans, cats suffer from diabetes when their metabolic system cannot effectively control amount of sugar in their blood stream. The main cause of this is usually lack of or limited production of insulin, which is produced in the pancreas. Apart from insufficient amount of insulin, your cat is at risk of developing diabetes in case it is obese, approaching old age, is a male, stressed, poor diet and hormonal imbalances.

Diabetes presents several symptoms including excessive thirst, rapid weight loss, loss of appetite, vomiting, increased urination and general body weakness among other symptoms.

Once diagnosed, your vet may recommend a number of ways to help your cat cope. One of the most effective ways your vet is most likely to recommend is diet, the kind of food you feed your cat on. A vegetarian diet with proper nutrient profile is usually very effective in managing diabetes in cats.

Gastrointestinal Disorders

These disorders also include disorders of a cat's digestive system. These are disorders that hinder smooth digestion and absorption of nutrients contained in the food that your cat eats. Gastrointestinal disorders in particular interfere with both the intestine and stomach causing pain and in some cases swelling. Some of these disorders include acute gastroenteritis, colitis, diarrhoea, constipation, irritable bowel syndrome and pancreatitis among others.

Occurrence of these disorders presents several symptoms including vomiting, flatulence, body weakness, constipation, diarrhoea and in some cases regurgitation.

Although they do not present any immediate danger, gastrointestinal and digestive disorders can become life-threatening if not addressed in good time. You need to take your cat to a vet for correct diagnosis and treatment. Treatment options available do aim at alleviating the pain and suffering that your cat experiences in addition to eliminating symptoms. One of the most effective treatment options available relates to the food that you feed your cat on. Vets do recommend highly digestible foods for cats with these conditions. Other recommended food types include high soluble foods.

You will be obligated to prevent occurrence of these disorders for the benefit of your cat. This will mean ascertaining specific factors or food stuffs that may be the cause of such disorders.

Heart Disease

Your Maine Coon cat is at risk of suffering from heart disease and like with most cat diseases, the food you feed your cat on plays a major role in preventing or encouraging the disease. There are however other factors that may cause heart disease in your cat including old age and heartworm among other factors.

Heart disease has the negative effect of enlarging your cat's heart, making it inefficient. In effect, the heart holds more fluid than it is supposed to hold. A clever way to go about preventing excessive fluid in your cat's heart is to feed it cat food low on sodium.

Heart disease presents several symptoms some similar to those presented by other cat diseases. These include low-pitched cough, difficulty in breathing, weight gain/loss and abdominal swelling among other symptoms.

Urinary Tract Infections

UTIs are various infections that do affect both the bladder and urethra. Of the infections, feline idiopathic cystitis (FIC) is the most prevalent. Thought to be caused by excessive level of stress, it causes inflammation of the urinary tract in addition to forming crystals along a cat's urinary tract. Such crystals are in most cases those of calcium oxalate.

Chapter 10 - Health

UTIs present different symptoms including inappropriate urination, straining during urination, loss of bladder control, coloured urine, licking of the genitals, loss of appetite and lack of interest in any activity among other symptoms.

UTIs can be caused by several factors including obesity, diet composed of foods rich in magnesium, calcium, phosphorous and protein (unbalanced), surgery and infections. Any UTI can be very problematic since occurrence rate remains high after treatment. This becomes real when causative factor is not addressed before treatment is offered. Vets emphasize on the need to feed your cat on the right cat food that is not only nutritious but also well balanced.

Obesity

Acquisition of food in the wild for any creature including cats is not an easy task. Cats in the wild have to literally hunt and chase after their prey to feed on. The physical exertion definitely takes a toll on their bodies and it is therefore not easy to find an obese cat in the wild. Things are however different for domesticated cats including Maine Coons. Domesticated cats have it very easy when it comes to food simply because all that they eat is readily provided, which poses the risk of obesity.

From study findings of a research study conducted by Association for Pet Obesity Prevention (APOP) in 2011, over 50% of cats in the USA were found to be either obese or overweight. It therefore simply means that your Maine Coon cat is also at risk of becoming obese even though it is one of the most active cat breeds you can find.

Simply put, your cat is most likely to become obese when its energy intake is more that the mount of energy it requires. Just like in humans, its body converts the extra energy it consumes into fat, which gets deposited in specific locations within its body.

Chapter 10 - Health

Getting rid of deposited fat can be a big challenge even with regulation of energy intake.

Living with an obese Maine Coon cat or any obese cat for that matter can be very expensive. This is so because obesity forms the foundation of a wide range of diseases and health conditions that will see you in and out of a vet's clinic on a regular basis. Just like in humans, obesity in cats causes such diseases as arthritis, heart disease, diabetes, cancer of the bladder and breathing difficulty.

The ideal weight of your Maine Coon cat should be between 15-26 pounds (7-12kg) and between 11-19 pounds (5-9 kg) for a male and female respectively. You need to take anything beyond these as a cause of concern. It is therefore important that you have your cat weighed whenever you call at the vet for regular check ups, which should ideally include weight measurement.

You should however be able to tell whether your cat is becoming obese or not even without weighing it. You should be able to feel your cat's backbone and ribs whenever you place your hand on its back. Failure to feel the bones should be a clear sign of obesity.

Obesity is a serious health condition in cats. Just like in humans, obesity in cats encourages occurrence of such serious diseases/health conditions as diabetes, heart disease and cardiovascular diseases. Ensuring that your Maine Coon cat maintains normal body weight goes a long way in preventing regular trips to a vet's clinic, which translates to reduced health care costs.

Your cat can become obese for several reasons one of which is free feeding. Most cats left free to choose when to eat often develop obesity. This is so because a free feeding program gives a cat the opportunity to overeat, in effect consuming too much food that its body does not really need. Veterinarians recommend

Chapter 10 - Health

---

feeding your adult cat between two to three meals in a day with amount of each meal controlled to avoid overeating. Ideally, your cat's food should be about half of human meal.

The other main cause of obesity in cats is intake of too much calories. Unlike humans, your cat does not have the Amylase enzyme that digests carbohydrates contained in their food. The enzyme plays the very important role of breaking down large carbohydrate molecules into smaller absorbable units of glucose.

Furthermore, cats are not carbohydrate consumers by nature. Because most dry cat foods contain high levels of carbohydrates, you need to shop carefully for the same. Any dry cat food you buy should have minimal carbohydrates if any. It is highly recommended that you feed your cat a diet that is similar to its natural food, which makes canned cat food stuffs better. A cat's ideal diet should be high on meat-based protein and moderate fat and water.

Apart from carbohydrates and free feeding program, the other main cause of obesity in cats is cat treat. Availability of cat treats has made many cat owners lazy when it comes to feeding their cats. Many cat owners rely on cat treats as their cats' main food. Cat treats contain high levels of carbohydrates and feeding your cat on the same on a regular basis puts it at great risk of becoming obese. You should only feed your cat on treats at special occasions as away of appreciation or reward.

Unlike in humans, obesity in cats is a non-hereditary health condition. Your cat will only develop obesity because of what you feed it on. It is therefore very necessary that you pay attention to what your cat eats and in what amounts.

Apart from food, you seriously need to ensure that your cat is physically engaged on a daily basis. Exercises are very important not only for your cat's physique but also in stimulating its mind.

Chapter 10 - Health

You need to make effective use of cat toys to help your cat burn excess fat deposits in the body.

Formulating a balanced and nutritious weight loss diet should also be effective in helping your cat cut down on excess body weight just in case it has already become obese. You need to formulate a diet that is low on carbohydrates but high on meat-based protein and other nutrients including fresh drinking water.

Pustule

Pustule in cats is what acne is to humans. Just like in humans who suffer acne mostly on the facial area, your cat is also likely to suffer acne that affects its chin although its lower lip can also be affected. Major causes of pustule in cats happen to be poor grooming (lack of it) and excess oil on the skin surface, oil produced from within the body.

Just like acne in humans, your cat is most likely to present such symptoms as black/whiteheads, swollen chin and development of nodules that can be very painful. Your cat can end up having boils as a result of pustule. A vet will normally try to rule out such health issues as feline leprosy, allergy and skin tumour before diagnosing pustule. Confirmation of correct diagnosis is usually through such procedures as fungal culture, biopsy test and skin scrapping among other procedures.

For treatment, a vet will normally prescribe antibiotics, topical creams and shampoos. Regular occurrence of pustules should be a cause of concern regarding your cat's general health. It may be necessary for a vet to undertake your cat's full health scan to ascertain the exact cause of the same.

Hypoadrenocorticism

This is what is commonly referred to as Addison's disease even in humans. This disease is mostly caused by imbalance in the levels of both glucocorticoid (cortisol) and mineralocorticoids (aldosterone,) hormones produced in the adrenal gland. These two hormones play the very important role of maintaining your cat's good health and excess or insufficient production of the same leads to serious health complications. Excess or insufficient production of the two hormones impairs the function of the kidney, gastrointestinal system, the nervous system and the cardiovascular system.

You cat will present a number of symptoms, which may include signs of depression, vomiting, bloody faeces, unexplained weight loss, general body weakness and lack of appetite among other symptoms. Apart from excess or insufficient production of the two hormones, the disease can also be caused by metastatic tumours.

A vet will normally perform elaborate laboratory tests, blood count and urinalysis test in diagnosing if your cat suffers from Addison's disease. If so, he/she may recommend that your cat remains hospitalized for intensive therapy since Addison's disease is usually an emergency case. The first line of treatment is usually giving of body fluids intravenously with the aim of balancing the two hormones. Your cat will henceforth need to receive hormonal treatment throughout its life even with recovery.

Feline Asthma/Bronchitis

This is the inflammation of a cat's bronchi and bronchioles, which leads to narrowing of airwaves. Left untreated, asthma/bronchitis presents the risk of a cat developing excess tissue within its lungs, tissues that make it very difficult for the lungs to inflate.

In both acute and chronic asthma/bronchitis cases, a cat is most likely to present such symptoms as coughing, body weakness, general body weakness, lack of appetite, breathing difficulties and skin coloration among other symptoms.

Although the exact cause of asthma/bronchitis in cats is yet to be known, your cat is most likely to suffer the same in case you smoke in the house, in which case your cat inhales the resultant smoke. The disease has also been linked to parasitic lung infection and in particular infection by lungworm, use of air fresheners at home and indoor chemical sprays.

Diagnosis of asthma/bronchitis in cats is usually through blood tests that also show whether it is acute or chronic. A vet may also need your cat's faecal sample to ascertain presence of parasites. There are instances when a vet may order for X-ray imaging with the aim of ascertaining both the nature and extent of the disease.

Asthma/bronchitis in cats is usually a serious disease and your cat will most likely be given Oxygen therapy in addition to anti-inflammatory medications to reduce swelling of the airwaves. A vet may recommend that your cat remains hospitalized for further investigation and monitoring.

Tyzzer Disease

This is a disease that mostly affects both kittens and young cats. It is a serious life-threatening disease caused by Clostridium piliformis bacterium that multiplies within the intestines before entering a cat's liver, leading to serious damage of the liver.

If infected, your cat will show a number of symptoms including general body weakness, signs of depression, loss of appetite, diarrhoea, low body temperature and abdominal distension among other symptoms.

Veterinarians do diagnose Tyzzer disease through laboratory tests of blood, urinalysis and blood count among other diagnosis procedures. Diagnosis of the disease is usually revealed when there is high level of liver enzymes. There is no treatment for Tyzzer disease and affected cats do die.

Chapter 10 - Health

Capillariasis

This is a cat disease caused by Capillaria plica and Capillaria feliscati, parasitic worms. Although the parasites mostly affect a cat's urinary bladder, it can also affect its urinary tract. Your cat will most likely show signs of frequent urination that can be painful, bloody urine and straining when urinating.

Diagnosis of this disease is through urinalysis, which should reveal presence of Capillaria ova. A vet may offer injection or other form of medications for treatment. The possibility of the disease recurring usually remains high especially if your cat is fond of venturing outdoors often. This is because it is outdoors where it has access to earthworms.

Hepatic Lipidosis

This is a disease of the liver that is commonly referred to as fatty liver. It is one of the most fatal diseases that affect domestic cats across the world. The liver plays the important roles of synthesizing proteins, producing digestive enzymes and detoxifying the body.

By its nature, a cat's liver cannot convert large amounts of fat into energy the way it is in humans. Failure by a cat's liver to convert large amounts of fat efficiently leads to accumulation of fat, which impairs the liver's function. Furthermore, the liver releases the accumulated fat that by then has turned yellow into the bloodstream, leading to yellowish eyes. Left untreated, a cat develops several health complications before dying of the disease.

Fatty liver can be caused by various health conditions and diseases including cancer, diabetes, kidney disease, inflammation of the pancreas and obesity, among others. If affected, your cat will most likely present such symptoms as yellowish eyes, unexplained rapid weight loss, signs of depression, jaundice, vomiting, constipation and drooling of saliva.

A vet will normally perform routine laboratory tests of blood count, urinalysis and biochemistry profile in diagnosing the disease. Such other imaging tools as radiography may also be performed to examine the abdomen. Your cat will most likely be hospitalized for treatment, which includes fluid therapy and vitamin B supplementation. A vet will obviously recommend an appropriate diet for your cat so as to prevent re-occurrence of the disease.

Sporotrichosis

This is a disease caused by Sporothrix schenckii fungus found in mould and yeast. Your cat can easily contract the fungus when it rubs against a surface with mould or yeast, in which case the fungus attaches to its skin before penetrating into the body. Your cat can also contract the disease when it inhales fumes from moulds.

If infected, your cat will most likely present such symptoms as skin lesions, swollen lymph glands and wounds on the head among other symptoms. This is a zoonotic disease that can be transmitted from human to animals and vice versa. It is therefore very important that you be careful when outdoors with your cat. In particular, your cat should not venture into areas with decaying organic matter.

In addition to physical examination, a vet will normally carry out laboratory fluid tests to diagnose the disease. Your cat will most likely be hospitalized for treatment that includes administration of anti-fungal medications.

Feline Trichobezoars

This is what is referred to as hairballs. Although it is perfectly normal for your cat to occasionally vomit a hairball, persistent and frequent vomiting of the hairballs is usually a sign of a serious health problem.

Chapter 10 - Health

The only evidence that your cat vomits hairballs is when you see the hairballs. These are masses of hair that are cylindrically shaped. They can form in your cat's stomach and only vomits them out when it regurgitates.

The cause of hairballs is directly linked to how cats groom themselves. Your cat's tongue is designed in such a way that it is barbed, which makes it possible for it to groom itself with ease. In the process of grooming itself, it swallows some of the hair it removes. It is this hair that accumulates in the stomach that it vomits or regurgitates.

Frequent vomiting or regurgitation of hairballs calls for veterinary attention. A vet should ideally perform such tests as blood cell count, biochemistry profile and thyroid screening among other tests to diagnose hairballs.

Hairball treatment usually involves lubricating the hairballs in the stomach to make it easy for a cat to pass the same out with faeces. A vet can also recommend feeding your cat some cat foods that are commercially available, foods that control accumulation of hair in the stomach. The best way to prevent your cat having hairballs is to groom it regularly.

Polyphagia

Polyphagia simply refers to a cat's increased appetite for food. It is a health condition where your cat simply starts demanding more food to the extent of becoming ravenous all the time. This condition can be caused by many factors and it is only appropriate that you ascertain the exact cause. Although your cat may gain weight, weight loss will be a sign that it is not well health wise.

In addition to increased appetite, your cat will most likely develop obesity or lose weight. Causes include onset of aging process, use of certain cat medications, diabetes and poor absorption of food.

Polyphagia is normally diagnosed through blood, urine tests and radiography imaging. Treatment normally takes into account the causative factor, which in case of a disease requires a vet to advices on the best management regime while treating the initial disease (causative factor).

Panosteitis

Panosteitis refers to inflammation of bones in cats. It is a very painful health condition that affects the long bones found in a cat's legs. If affected, your cat will most likely limp before becoming lame. Although this condition mostly affects large-sized cats including Maine Coons, it can also affect medium-sized cats. It is however a treatable health condition that a cat can recover from to lead a perfectly normal life.

In addition to limping, your cat is also most likely to show such other symptoms as signs of depression, fever, anorexia and weight loss among other symptoms. While actual cause of this health condition remains unknown, diagnosis is through X-ray imaging and blood tests. Treatment of this health condition is usually limited to pain management in which case a vet is bound to prescribe anti-inflammatory and steroid medications.

Inflammatory Bowel Disease (IBD)

IBD is a term used to refer to several diseases and health conditions that affect a cat's gastrointestinal tract and whose cause(s) remain largely unknown. One characteristic of all the diseases is that they cause inflammation of the intestines.

Your cat will present several symptoms if affected. Some of these include diarrhoea, signs of depression, flatulence, abdominal pain, general body weakness, bloody stool and distressed hair on the coat.

Diagnosis of IBD is normally through laboratory tests including blood count, biochemistry profile and urinalysis. Although cure for IBD is not available, a vet will normally institute control measures that include stabilization of body weight, reduction of immune system response and administration of antibiotic medications.

Coprophagia

This is a health condition that normally worries cat owners. Your cat may suddenly start eating its own faeces after defecating. Although the actual cause of this condition is unknown, it is thought to be as a result of both mineral and vitamin deficiency in a cat's diet.

Apart from eating its faeces, you may also observe your cat eating rocks, clay and soap among other non-edible items. Your cat will also diarrhoea and vomit frequently.

Apart from mineral and vitamin deficiency, other factors believed to cause the condition include malnutrition and such other diseases as thyroid disease, diabetes and increased appetite among other factors.

Diagnosing this health condition can be very involving. A vet will normally set out to ascertain whether the condition is a simple behavioral problem or a medical condition, in which case he/she will undertake a complete biochemistry profile, blood count and urinalysis. Treating this condition depends on causative factor. While change of your cat's environment may help in case the causative factor is ascertained to behavioral, a vet may prescribe specific medications should the causative factor be medically related.

Urine Incontinence

This is a case of lack of control of the bladder, just in the same way it is in humans. Your cat will present different symptoms in case it has this health condition. Such include frequent urination, wet hair between its rear legs or on the abdomen, skin inflammation around its genitals and wet beddings among other symptoms.

There are simply many factors that can make your cat loose control of its bladder. Some of these include neutering/spaying procedures that disrupt the nerves around the bladder, lesions on the brain, overactive bladder syndrome, UTIs, lesions on the spinal cord and underdevelopment of the bladder among many other causes.

Diagnosing urine incontinence in cats can be very challenging because of the many possible causes. A vet will however strive to ascertain the particular cause before designing an effective treatment plan that may take some time. Treatment normally depends on the ascertained cause.

Mesothelioma

Mesothelioma refers to a rare type of tumour that develops on the cellular tissue lining the interior part of a cat's body, the epithelial linings. These linings play the important role of protecting the internal organs by covering them. They also facilitate movement within the body.

Just like with other types of tumour, Mesothelioma develops when mesothelial cells fail to divide or replicate in the normal way before migrating to other parts of the body, which further spreads the tumour.

Your cat will show several symptoms if affected including difficulty in breathing, muffled lung/heart sounds, general body weakness, vomiting, inability to exercise and enlarged abdomen among other symptoms.

Diagnosing this condition normally involves a vet undertaking a complete blood profile, blood count and urinalysis. A vet may also obtain X-ray image of your cat's abdomen/chest, radiography and ultrasound to observe presence of masses in the body cavities. Drainage of unnecessary fluids within the body is usually the first line of treatment before medications are prescribed.

Stertor/Stridor

While Stertor refers to a cat's low-pitched noisy breathing, Stridor refers to the high-pitched noisy breathing that your Maine Coon cat can exhibit. Stertor is most likely to occur when your cat inhales air. It is similar to snoring except that your cat's inhalation of air will be constricted, resulting in a low-pitched breathing occasioned by vibration of tissues that align the throat. On the other hand, Stridor is likely to occur when your cat inhales air with throat tissues in a rigid state.

Your cat will exhibit a number of symptoms when affected. These include inability to meow and extra-ordinary nature of breathing among other symptoms. These two related conditions can be caused by narrowed nostrils, inverted laryngeal, paralysis of the voice box/windpipe, tumour of the voice box and presence of foreign matter within the windpipe.

There are also risk factors associated with occurrence of the two health conditions. Some of these include an environment with high temperatures, high metabolic rate, over-exercising and poor drinking/eating habits among other possible risk factors. Diagnosis of the two conditions usually involves a vet obtaining your cat's health history, perform internal imaging procedure (fluoroscopy) and X-ray imaging of the neck to identify any abnormalities in the neck's soft tissues. There are instances where a vet may need to perform surgery when foreign matter is lodged within the windpipe.

Baylisascarisis

This is what is referred to as Raccoon disease in cats. The disease also affects humans. It is transmitted by larvae of Baylisascarisis procyyonis parasite (roundworm) found in faeces left open in the environment. Your cat is most likely to contract the larvae in case it is used to venturing outdoors into areas with other cats having the parasite. Your cat will present several symptoms if affected. These include un-coordinated walking, difficulty in swallowing, regular seizures and general confusion among other symptoms.

Diagnosis of this disease is through laboratory examination of faecal smear test that should detect presence of the disease in your cat's intestines. The larvae should be seen through ophthalmoscopic examination. There are a good number of medications that a vet can prescribe for your cat including Corticosteroids and albendazole medications.

Abscess

Abscess refers to skin irritation. Just like in humans, cats also suffer from skin irritation. Although simple skin irritation can be treated using topical creams and ointments, serious cases of irritation can worsen especially when bacteria invades affected area.

Skin irritation can be caused by a number of factors including fights with other cats, fights from which infected cats infect your cat with Pasteurella multocida bacteria, which causes skin irritation. Left untreated, the bacterium finds its way deep into the skin, causing other internal problems.

In treating skin irritation, a vet will normally recommend use of topical skin creams/ointments as the first line of treatment. This can be in addition to antibiotics. A vet may undertake clindamycin treatment in case of serious skin irritation where the bacterium has penetrated the skin.

Hematuria

This refers to a condition where your cat's urine contains blood. This can be a serious disease since it may be a sign of a serious underlying process. One of the serious underlying diseases that cause hematuria is cancer. In most cases, female cats stand a high risk of suffering hematuria compared to male cats.

Apart from cancer, there are many other factors that can cause hematuria. These include low level of platelets in the blood, UTS's, kidney disease, anatomic disease and other metabolic diseases among other causes.

Vets do treat hematuria as emergency cases. It is therefore very important that you take your cat to a vet the first instance you notice your cat passing urine containing blood.

Idiopathic Epilepsy

This is seizures in cats. It is a disorder that occurs in a cat's brain and causes sudden and in almost all cases uncontrolled/recurring attacks. If affected, your cat may or may not loose consciousness. Your cat will normally have a short aura and look as if it is under threat. It will eventually fall on its side at the onset of attack and may salivate, defecate or urinate. An attack can last between 20 and 90 seconds before it recovers.

Seizures can occur when your cat is awake or when it is a sleep. The period soon after an attack is usually followed by such behaviour as general confusion, blindness, increased thirst, increased appetite and aimless wondering among other abnormal behaviour.

The exact cause(s) of idiopathic epilepsy remains largely unknown although it has been proved to be a hereditary health condition. Diagnosis of the condition normally involves blood cell count, thyroid screening and testing for viral infections if any.

Chapter 10 - Health

Treatment of this condition normally involves administration of anticonvulsant medications.

Constipation/Obstipation

Constipation is a condition where your cat finds it hard to defecate. The condition is characterized by incomplete, infrequent and defecation difficulty. On the other hand, Obstipation refers to worsened constipation. It is pronounced constipation characterized by lack of bowel movement, in which case a cat does not defecate at all.

You can easily tell when your cat has constipation. Apart from straining when defecating, it will also loose appetite. You may also notice swelling around the anus. Your cat is also most likely to produce hard and dry faeces with very little amount of urine.

Defecation can be caused by various factors including swallowed hair, swallowed bones, excess fibre in your cat's food, lack of exercise and low blood calcium among many other factors. It is very important that you do not allow constipation to develop further into Obstipation. It may be necessary to take your cat to a vet who will be able to undertake proper diagnosis of cause.

Treating constipation depends on the cause. A vet may recommend dietary supplementation or rehydration. A vet may also undertake manual removal of faeces in case of Obstipation. Surgery may be the only option in case of serious Obstipation. It is very important that you regularly monitor your cat's stool with the aim of detecting constipation in good time.

Hematoma/Seroma

Hematoma refers to a condition where blood collects in one spot outside blood vessels. On the other hand, Seroma refers to the same, except that the collected blood does not contain any red blood cells, it is purely serum. Both hematoma and Seroma can occur in any part of your cat's body including within the ears and brain. The most common happen to be sub-dermal hematoma/Seroma that develops just under the cat's skin.

The symptoms that hematoma/Seroma present depend on area of the body affected. Symptoms for sub-dermal hematoma/Seroma include swelling under the skin and itchiness around the area.

Hematoma/Seroma that develops in the head or brain presents such symptoms as seizures and coma. Hematoma/Seroma can be caused by various factors including trauma and in some cases serious insect bites.

It is very important that you give your cat a thorough physical examination when bathing. Doing so makes it possible to detect any unusual symptoms that may be of sub-dermal hematoma. A vet should be able to carry out physical and other tests on blood/serum drawn from affected part for proper diagnosis. A vet can also perform imaging tests including X-ray, ultrasound, CT and MRI to diagnose internal hematoma/Seroma.

While minor hematoma/Seroma do re-absorb and resolve on their own without any medication, a vet is obligated to undertake treatment procedures to resolve serious cases. Treatment involves draining the collected blood/serum and surgery in case of internal hematoma/Seroma.

Accidents

Although all cats are susceptible to accidents, Maine Coons stand greatest risk of getting involved in other forms of accidents than those related heights. This is because Maine Coons are not fond of heights even though they at times climb. It is therefore very important that you make your home as cat friendly as possible by removing any sharp objects on the floor that they can fall on. Serious injuries require that you take your cat to a vet at the earliest possible time since the same can be life-threatening.

Chapter 10 - Health

Signs of Illness

Diseases do not develop overnight. It takes time before your cat finally falls ill. You need to be able to notice when your cat starts to show abnormal behaviour even before it falls ill. You can only do this having interacted and socialized with your cat to a point where you can easily tell when it is about to fall ill. Signs of illness in cats can be categorized into two; behavioural and physical signs.

Behavioural Signs

You should be able to notice different unusual behaviour by your cat, behaviour that should prompt you to take your cat to a vet at the earliest possible opportunity unless you know the reason for any unusual behaviour.

Although your cat will avoid its litter box when the box is unclean, avoidance of the same is usually a clear sign of a medical condition. Urination outside the litter box can be a sign of such medical conditions as diabetes, urinary tract infection or kidney failure. You need to take your cat to a vet in case you notice this unusual behaviour more than once when the litter box is perfectly clean.

Cats generally are not fond of drinking water. They obtain the water they need from their food. Although your cat will occasionally drink water, increased intake of water should be a cause of concern. This will be a sign of thirst, which is usually a sign of such health conditions/diseases as diabetes and hyperthyroidism among other diseases.

Failure by your cat to eat as it normally does should be a serious cause of concern. This may be an indication of loss of appetite that may in turn be a sign of many diseases including gingivitis, trauma or anaemia among many other diseases.

Interacting and socializing with your cat should make it possible for you to know when and why it meows. Excess meowing

Chapter 10 - Health

(vocalization) may be a sign of stress, fear, sickness, pain or other medical condition.

Your cat is most likely to spend a better part of the day and in particular during the morning hours sleeping. Although this is perfectly normal, excessive sleep in addition to hiding when it is a wake should be a sign of fear, anxiety or sickness.

Being people-oriented, your Maine Coon cat will most likely get into the habit of welcoming you whenever you arrive at home. You will need to be concerned with any change in this habit. You will need to establish where your cat goes when not welcoming you. It is most likely that you will find your cat in its litter box, which should alert you of a medical problem.

Physical Signs

Unlike behavioural signs of sickness, physical signs are easy to notice and one of the most obvious signs you should be able to notice is a change in your cat's coat appearance. The fact that cats generally groom themselves means that your cat's coat should always be smooth. You should be concerned when the coat appears ruffled, which may be a sign of malnutrition, parasitic infection or such other skin disorders as ringworm or allergy.

Your cat should always have good breath. Bad breath will definitely not be normal since such may be a sign of diabetes, gingivitis, kidney disease or gastrointestinal disorder among other diseases/health conditions.

Any rapid weight loss or gain should be a serious concern. This is so because such may be a sign of many health conditions including malnutrition, overfeeding, diabetes, kidney failure or heart disease among many others.

Chapter 10 - Health

When to Visit a Vet

Regardless of your Maine Coon cat's age, five very important factors determine how healthy it will be; proper nutrition and weight management, environment, good dental care, parasite control and vaccinations. The food that you feed your cat on determines whether or not it will remain healthy throughout its lifetime. You also need to make your cat's environment as friendly as possible to allow it to enjoy its life to the fullest. Ensure that you do not only socialize with your cat but engage in play activities as well.

Ensuring that your cat's oral health is at its optimum will also go a long way in preventing many diseases. Closely related to environment is the issue of parasites. Note that parasites thrive in unhygienic locations and it is therefore very necessary to ensure that your cat's room or space remains clean all the time. Lastly, you need to ensure that your cat receives all the recommended vaccinations and any other vaccination that may be fronted by relevant authorities from time to time.

When to take your cat to a vet depends on its age. Although kittens are in most cases sold off when they have already received the most important vaccinations, you will need to take yours to a vet at least three times in a year for any additional vaccinations or routine check ups. Doing so will make it possible for you to know any health issues that your kitten may have once it comes of age.

An adult Maine Coon cat does not require too much vet attention so long as you feed it on recommended foods and keep its environment clean. Your adult cat will have received the recommended vaccinations and should be in a position to remain healthy for a long time. You will however need to take it to a vet at least twice in a year for routine check ups.

Having an old or aging cat can be a little of a problem because of the many visits you may need to make to a vet clinic. This is because it is during old age that such age-related diseases/health conditions as arthritis and heart disease among others set in. You will need to take your aging cat to a vet at least three times in a year for routine medical check ups and for such indicated diseases/health conditions.

Your cat's general health remains squarely in your hands. You should take every step possible to ensure that your cat is not at risk of contracting any disease. You should be in a position to perform at-home physical examinations on a regular basis with the aim of determining your cat's general health condition. Although you need to take your kitten, cat or aging cat to a vet as indicated, there are instances when it becomes necessary to take it to a vet at the earliest opportunity possible. Such incidents as accidents require that you take your cat to a vet for immediate medical attention.

The Veterinarian

The professionals commonly referred to as veterinarians or vets in short are actually veterinary physicians trained to treat diseases, disorders and injuries that affect non-human animals. Vets are referred to as differently in different countries around the world. Although they are generally referred to as vets, they are professionally referred to as veterinary surgeons in the UK for instance.

Different countries have strict legislations when it comes to veterinary services, just the same way it is with human physicians. It is mandatory in almost all countries for anyone using the term a vet to have undertaken the necessary training, registered and licensed to practice as a vet. Vets work in many institutions. There are those who work in vet clinics where they engage with animal owners or pet owners directly in treating their livestock. There are also those who work in such institutions as zoos, research institutions and animal hospitals.

Chapter 10 - Health

Just in the same way that human doctors specialize in a specific area, vets also specialize. You are therefore most likely to come across a vet who is a surgery or dermatology specialist or one specializing in internal medicine. Generally however, vets diagnose and treat non-human diseases and health conditions in addition to providing aftercare and administration of vaccines.

It is common practice to find vets in different countries working in the private sector. Only a small number work in government institutions. The fact that majority work in the private sectors and in particular in clinics allows them to work directly with animal owners, owners whose animals have varied diseases and health conditions.

The fact that you plan to buy or already own a cat and a Maine Coon cat for that matter will obviously make it necessary to pay a vet a visit. This can be on the first day when you bring the cat home for the requisite vaccine(s). Just like with choosing your personal physician, you need to carefully choose a vet to engage for your cat's treatment and administration of vaccines.

How to Find a Vet

The fact that most vets work in clinics and private clinics makes finding the best vet a big challenge. This can be very true in case you live in a location where there are many practicing vets. The first way to finding the right vet is to enquire from close family members, neighbours and friends with pets. They should be able to refer you to a vet they personally know and who provides quality service.

Apart from making enquiries, you also have the option of consulting your local professional organization for information on licensed vets practicing in your locality. You also have the option of getting information on the right vets from a local cat breeder. A breeder in particular will be better placed to refer you to the right vet because he/she obviously engages the service of a vet to treat his/her cats in the cattery.

Chapter 10 - Health

Whether you choose to make enquiries or contact a professional organization or a cat breeder, there are certainly several issues you will need to ascertain before you engage the service of a vet and one of these issues is whether or not the vet is licensed and enjoys some accreditation. A professional and ethical vet will normally share with you his certification, which should ideally be posted on the office wall. You will also need to ascertain whether or not the vet is a member of a local professional organization.

Apart from a vet's certification, accreditation and level of experience, you need to undertake an overall assessment of the facility with knowledge that it is at that clinic where you will hence forth be bringing your Maine Coon cat in case of health problems. It is therefore important to assess a facility's level of cleanliness among other issues.

It is common for vets to enter into agreements with pet owners for the purpose of taking care of their pets' health. Although most pet owners are in favour of such agreements as one way of cutting down on their pets' health care costs, doing so can be costly without due diligence.

It is possible that you and your pet's vet can have disagreements that force you to engage the service of a different vet. Terminating an agreement can be very costly depending on agreement period you agreed upon. The best way to cutting down on your cat's health care costs is to shop for a suitable pet insurance policy that covers risks that your cat is susceptible to.

Cat Insurance

Your Maine Coon cat is not only people friendly; it turns out to be the best companion you can have at home as a pet. Furthermore, it makes you active because of its playful nature. It is definitely a valuable family member. Just in the same way that you ensure your other family members are comfortable and in good health, you need to ensure that your cat also remains in good

Chapter 10 - Health

health and one way to go about this is to take out cat insurance for your Maine Coon.

It is a fact that veterinary fees and medication costs are always on the rise, which can make it impossible for you to meet your cat's medical costs at a time it needs it most. Taking out appropriate cat insurance policy goes a long way in keeping your veterinary costs low while giving your cat good health care.

Regardless of your location, any cat insurance policy you are likely to find is designed to cover the cost of veterinary fees and treatment of diseases/health conditions and injuries. Although very important, choosing the right cat insurance policy for your cat can be a big challenge. This is because there are simply many policies out there in the market that differ in terms of what they cover and price. This makes it necessary to know the best time to take out cat insurance.

The best time to take out cat insurance is when your cat is young, a kitten. This is because age is one of the most important factors pet insurance companies take into consideration when determining the level of insurance premium to quote. Kittens generally attract low premium rates compared to adult and aging cats that attract high premium rates because of various factors including onset of age-related diseases/health conditions.

There are generally four types of cat insurance policies you can choose from; lifetime, maximum benefit, limited time and accident-only policies.

Lifetime cat insurance policy covers vet fees for one year. You will need to continuously renew the policy to enjoy the same cover at the same premium rate regardless of how many claims you make. Although the cost of this policy is usually on the higher side, it is beneficial taking into account the fact that your cat remains covered for its lifetime even when it develops life-long disease.

Chapter 10 - Health

Unlike the lifetime policy, the maximum benefit policy provides cover for a pre-determined maximum amount of veterinary fees per health condition. The specific health condition is considered a pre-existing condition and is therefore excluded from future claims once the maximum limit is reached.

The time limited policy is similar to the maximum benefit policy except that the latter is limited to one year only, a period in which vet fees can be offset for each health condition.

The accident-only policy is limited to treatment of injuries your cat may sustain from accidents at home or outside the home including on the road.

A common feature of almost all cat insurance policies is the exclusion of pre-existing medical conditions. Such other procedures as preventative treatments, pregnancy/birth, neutering/spaying and worm control are also excluded from the policies. It is very important that you undertake some little research with the aim of finding a pet insurance company that quotes low premium rates on policies that provide a specific cover you need for your Maine Coon cat.

Chapter 11 – Vaccinations

What is a Vaccine?
A vaccine is basically a solution containing antigens that to the body's immune system looks like disease-causing organism but is not. Your cat can be given a vaccine orally or through injection. When introduced into the body, the vaccine stimulates the body's complex immune system, making the system strong enough to fight any disease-causing organism that enters the body. Having your cat vaccinated is therefore very important.

Different jurisdictions have different vaccine requirements for all pets including cats. While some vaccines are only available in particular regions of the world because of prevalence of specific cat diseases, others are only available in other regions. There are basically two types of vaccines; core and non-core vaccines. While core vaccines are mandatory to all cats regardless of region or location, non-core vaccines are only found in specific regions or locations.

Like with anything introduced into the body, vaccines present several symptoms including fever, vomiting, loss of appetite, sluggishness, diarrhoea and swelling around injection area. There are also serious symptoms that may occur depending on the kind of vaccine your cat receives. These include life-threatening allergic reactions and development of tumour around injected area. The serious symptoms are however limited in occurrence. Vaccine symptoms are generally mild and do fade away within a fed days.

Safety of Vaccines
Although cat vaccines are generally safe, there has been controversy around some vaccines that are often considered

Chapter 11 - Vaccinations

---

unnecessary. You need to appreciate the fact that it is because of feline vaccines that cats can now live beyond their expected lifespan. Production and administration of most vaccines that had raised controversies have luckily ceased. It is therefore perfectly safe to take your Maine Coon cat to a vet to receive the core vaccines. In any case, you are most likely to buy a Maine Coon kitten that is already vaccinated.

One major challenge that many cat owners face is when to have their cats vaccinated. There are different circumstances and instances when your cat needs to be vaccinated.

Kitten Vaccination

Your Maine Coon kitten or cat is most likely to have received its first vaccination while still with the breeder you bought it from. Even so, the vaccination must have been several weeks after it was born. This is because kittens naturally acquire sufficient immunity from their mothers through milk. Furthermore, a kitten's immune system is still not yet fully developed to receive artificial vaccination.

Breeders do arrange with veterinarians for their kittens to be vaccinated once they attain the age of seven weeks with additional vaccinations administered when they are twelve and again once they attain the age of sixteen years. The two additional vaccinations are in most cases boosters that fortify the first vaccination.

Adult Cat Immunization

Adult cats are not vaccinated but rather immunized. Like with vaccination, immunization is aimed at further boosting your cat's immune system to continue being effective in offering protection against possible infections.

Core Cat Vaccines

Core cat vaccines are those that all cats should receive regardless of location. These vaccines are very effective in offering protection against life-threatening diseases found in all regions of the world. They include:

Feline Viral Rhinotracheitis (FVR) Vaccine
FVR Vaccine is administered to protect against FVR virus that is at times referred to as feline influenza or feline pneumonia. This is a respiratory disease found across the globe.

FVR is a highly contagious disease that can kill kittens within a few days of infection. The disease is easily transmitted through direct contact. One cat passes the disease on to another cat through saliva, nasal and eye secretions. When infected, your cat will most likely show such signs as coughing, sneezing, excessive nasal discharge, loss of appetite and high fever.

Feline Calicivirus (FCV) Vaccine
Your cat receives this vaccination to protect itself against the virus that causes respiratory infection. Occurrence of this disease usually ends in epidemic in areas with large cat population because of its highly contagious nature.

FCV presents such symptoms as nose/eye discharge, mouth ulceration, anorexia and general body weakness at the initial stage. If affected, your cat is most likely to present such secondary symptoms as jaundice, high fever, swelling of the face and limbs (oedema) and dysfunction of organs within the body.

Feline Panleukopenia Virus (FPV) Vaccine
FPV vaccine is one of the most important cat vaccines that your cat must receive. This is because the vaccine offers protection against the highly contagious and fatal diseases caused by Panleukopenia virus that causes low white blood cells. The disease is largely transmitted through contact with body fluids of an infected cat.

If infected, your cat is most likely to show signs of severe dehydration, bloody diarrhoea, anaemia, depression, vomiting, loss of appetite, self-biting and loss of skin elasticity among other signs. Pregnant cats affected by the disease do give birth to kittens with cerebellar hypopasia.

Feline Immunodeficiency Virus (FIV) Vaccine
FIV is often referred to as feline AIDS. This is so because it is in many ways similar to human immunodeficiency virus (HIV). There are different types of FIV that the FIV Vaccine is designed to protect against. Like in humans, your cat is most likely to live with FIV in case of infection in which case it will now be a carrier of the virus.

FIV attacks the immune system just in the same way that HIV does in humans. Although FIV and HIV are similar, humans cannot contract FIV and cats cannot contract HIV. Should your cat be infected, it will henceforth transmit the virus to other cats through saliva. Outdoor cats happen to be more at risk of contracting FIV virus compared to indoor cats.

Non-Core Cat Vaccines
Although classified as non-core cat vaccines, vaccines in this category are core in some regions of the world. This is because they are designed to offer cats protection against specific diseases only found in such regions. They include:

Feline Leukaemia Virus (FLV) Vaccine
FLV is a virus that causes life-threatening diseases in cats. One common disease associated with the virus is leukaemia, which develops when the virus destroys blood cells, in effect making them cancerous. The virus presents several symptoms including loss of appetite, poor coat condition, skin infections, fatigue, oral infections including gingivitis, diarrhoea and jaundice among many other symptoms. Your cat, if infected, will be able to transmit the virus to other cats through saliva, litter box (sharing) and food/water dishes.

Chapter 11 - Vaccinations

Rabies Vaccine
Rabies was in the past a universal medical condition that affected humans, dogs and other warm-blooded animals such as cats. Vaccination campaigns undertaken in specific regions of the world made it possible for the disease to be eradicated in such regions. Rabies vaccine is now only common in specific regions where cats, dogs and humans are still vulnerable to Rabies infection.

Rabies is a serious disease that you should protect your Maine Coon cat from by ensuring that it receives the necessary vaccination. It is a viral disease that causes serious inflammation of the brain. It presents such symptoms as fever, loss of consciousness and restricted movement among other symptoms. Most rabies cases do result in death.

Chlamydophila Felis Vaccine
Chlamydophila felis is a bacteria commonly found in cats. The vaccine for the bacteria is designed to protect against it. The bacteria cause inflammation of a cat's conjunctiva, rhinitis and respiratory health problems.

Depending on your location, you may be required from time to time to take your cat to a local vet for specific vaccinations aimed at preventing identified cat diseases in your specific area. Such vaccinations are in most cases occasioned by outbreak of cat diseases. Different countries have legislated legislations that make such vaccinations mandatory and failure to adhere to the same attracts different penalties.

Apart from being a requirement of legislation, you need to consider your cat's vaccination seriously. This is because you are the ultimate beneficiary knowing that your cat is fully vaccinated or immunized and therefore well protected from diseases that can affect its health. It is therefore very important that you consult your local vet on a regular basis for proper information on cat vaccinations and immunizations.

Chapter 12 - Costs

Chapter 12 – Costs

Owning a Maine Coon cat is simply fulfilling. Not only is it a pet but a valuable companion as well. However, being responsible for your lovely Maine Coon comes at a cost, which you are obligated to bear. Although maintaining a cat can be very expensive, you can keep maintenance costs low so long as you stick to feeding it on appropriate diet, ensuring that it receives all the necessary vaccinations/immunizations and maintaining proper hygiene at home.

You should be capable of maintaining your Maine Coon cat to make it different from any other Maine Coon cat or other cats on the street. Failure to meet some of your Maine Coon cat's needs and demands can easily be a cause of health problems. Furthermore, you stand the risk of losing your cat since it may simply run away onto the street.

There are different costs you are bound to incur when you plan to own and maintain a Maine Coon cat. You are most likely to incur heavy expenses when you prepare to buy or adopt one. Most of the costs relate to supplies that the cat will need soon after arriving at home. They include:

Food – There is no doubt that your cat will need to eat not just any food but quality cat food. This will be an incurring expense since you will need to buy quality food often. The cost of quality cat food averages $120 - $150 (£71- £89) per month depending on your location. Yearly maintenance costs on food will therefore be around $1,800 (£ 1,072) in any given year.

Nutrition Supplements – These are dietary supplements that you may need to buy for your Maine Coon. You will however need to

Chapter 12 - Costs

consult a vet before buying any. Ideally, it is a vet who should inform you when your cat needs supplements, which may be because of a special need. You may need to incur about $100 (£60) at any given time on dietary supplements.

Food/Water Bowls – These are supplies you will need to buy before you bring your kitten or cat home. Note that sharing of food/water bowls used by your cat will not be allowed. For instance, you should not feed your dog on the same food/water bowls used by your cat. Quality food/water bowls retail around $10 - $30 (£6 - £18) depending on your location. Note that you may need to replace the same at least twice in any given year, which makes yearly costs on food/water bowls between $60 - $90 (£35- £54).

Treats – Treats are edible food stuffs that you will need to feed your cat on once in a while. They are actually niceties that you use as rewards when your cat does something positive. You are most likely to offer your cat treats more often during the first few months as you subject it to training, in which case you are bound to incur between $30 and $100 (£18 - £60) per month. Yearly treat costs average between $60 and $300 (£35- £178).

Grooming Supplies – Like with all cats, the Maine Coon cat is naturally a clean cat that goes the extra mile to keep itself as clean as possible. It will therefore groom itself often to achieve this. You will however still need to groom your cat, in which case you will be obligated to invest in quality grooming supplies. While you are bound to spend around $50 - $100 (£30 - £60) in buying permanent grooming supplies such as tools, you will spend between $30 - $60 (£18 - £35) on such other recurrent supplies as shampoos and odour removers every month. Your cat's yearly grooming costs will average between $200 and $500 (£120 - £300).

Cat Bed – Your Maine Coon cat will need a good place to sleep in and investing in a quality cat bed is highly recommended. A cat

Chapter 12 - Costs

bed lasts a long time and you may only need to replace it when it is very necessary. A quality cat bed retails at between $20 and $100 (£12 - £60) depending on your location.

Cat Carrier – Like human babies, you will need to invest in a quality cat carrier for use in transporting your cat. Cats are generally not fond of travelling in cars and having a carrier makes travelling with your cat trouble-free. A quality cat carrier will set you financially back by between $20 and $100 (£12 - £60). You may only need to replace it after two or three years.

Cat Toys – Your cat is a playful and very active pet. This is why investing in quality cat toys is not only highly recommended but also very necessary. Having toys around will not only engage your cat in play but will also go a long way in helping it release a lot of energy it has, energy that if it would not use will make living with your cat a little bit of a problem. Quality cat toys retail at between $20 and $50 (£12 - £30) a piece and since you will need to buy different types, you should be ready to spend anything between $100 and $250 (£60 - £150) on toys once in a long time.

Scratching Post – Having a cat at home presents the risk of having your furniture scratched. This is because cats have a natural scratching instinct. The best way of dealing with the risk of having your furniture scratched is providing your cat with a scratching post, which costs between $50 and $100 (£30 - £60 only once.

Proper care of your Maine Coon is not limited to making food and the other supplies available. You also need to ensure that your cat is in good health. Veterinary service will therefore be very necessary, at a cost. There are different veterinary services your cat requires. They include:

Routine vet exams – These are routine vet exams a vet undertakes with the aim of determining your cat's health

Chapter 12 - Costs

condition. This can be three times in a year for a kitten, twice for an adult cat and thrice for an aging cat. You will be obligated to incur between $50 and $200 (£30 - £120 for such exams in any given year depending on your cat's age.

Vaccinations/Immunizations – Although you are most likely to adopt or buy a vaccinated kitten, there are immunizations it will need to receive once it comes of age. Such immunizations cost between $50 and $150 (£30 - £90) per year, depending on your location.

Spaying/Neutering – You may choose to have your cat spayed/neutered, in which case it will not be able to bring forth offspring. Having your cat spayed/neutered will cost you between $150 and $300 (£89 - £180), a one-off expense.

Emergency Care – You certainly will not rule out your cat getting injured, which will require emergency vet care. Depending on nature of injury and your location, you are most likely to incur between $500 and $2,000 (£300 - £1,190) on emergency care, which may involve surgery.

Veterinary costs can be huge to the extent that they exceed any other cat maintenance expenses. This is why many cat owners choose to buy cat insurance policies that cover risks that their cats are exposed to, something which you too may consider.

Maintaining your cat requires that you be ready to commit yourself financially for its overall well-being and health. On average, your Maine Coon cat's monthly maintenance cost will range between $400 and $700 (£238 - £416) and therefore around $1,500 - $5,000 (£890- £2980 in a year.

Maintaining a cat can indeed be a very expensive undertaking. There are however several ways through which you can cut down on maintenance expenses and one of these is buying cat food in bulk. You can cut on cat food expenses by almost 50% by simply

128

Chapter 12 - Costs

buying the same in bulk. The best way of realizing this is to buy in wholesale price, which guarantees you attractive discount.

Apart from cat food, cat treatment is the other recurrent expenditure you are most likely to incur throughout your cat's life. Taking your cat whenever it falls sick or when it gets injured and paying out of pocket can be very expensive. You need to consider taking out the best cat insurance for your cat. It will be appropriate to shop for a cat insurance policy that covers most of diseases and health conditions that your cat is susceptible to.

It is not mandatory to buy your cat's equipment including toys. You can effectively make use of locally available materials to make such equipment as scratch post, cat bed, cat tree and food/water dishes. You can make these as DIY projects or engage the service of a local artist to make them for you at a very minimal cost.

Chapter 13 – Caring for Your Aging Maine Coon

Major milestones have been achieved in the last decade or so when it comes to treatment of cat diseases and management of cat health conditions. Improvements of existing cat medications and discovery of new cat treatment methods has made it possible for cats to live much longer than their expected lifespan.

Although all cats of all ages benefit from such improvements, aging cats happen to be the biggest beneficiaries. This is because properly cared for aging cats can now age gracefully without necessarily experiencing the pain and a lot of discomfort that aging cats hitherto experienced in the past. Although your Maine Coon cat generally has a lifespan of 18 years, it can live to attain the age of 21 years so long as you provide it with proper care including veterinary care.

What is aging?
Aging is a process that every living being goes through. It is a natural process that sets in when life expectancy is attained, which in this case is 18 years for Maine Coon cat breed. One day in a cat's life is a very long time taking into account the fact that a year in a cat's life is similar to about 15 years for humans. Likewise, a cat aged 15 years is like a human being aged 85 years. Just like in humans, the onset of aging in cats brings with it several challenges, some which can make your cat very uncomfortable if you do not offer the necessary help.

Psychological & Behavioural Changes
Your Maine Coon will exhibit many changes once it attains old age. One of the most visible changes is the tendency to walk on

Chapter 13 - Caring for Your Aging Maine Coon

its hocks. This is because its hind leg muscles become weak to a point where running and jumping becomes difficult. This is the time to change its bed to a larger one because it finds it difficult to curl up in a small bed. Your aging cat will also be very forgetful. It may choose to remain outdoors in case it ventures out regardless of the weather. This is also the time when it can easily get lost in case it is used to venturing out without company.

A visible sign of aging in cats is usually what is referred to as winding down. This is when it grows thinner with its hip, shoulder and backbones becoming visible. In addition to becoming thinner, the fat layer just under the skin also melts away, further exposing the bones. It is important at this stage to consult a vet for advice on special types of cat food and dietary supplements to feed your cat on. The aging process also causes many faculty changes in a cat's life. Its hearing and cognition abilities diminish to a great extent. Furthermore, its metabolic rate also decreases. In case your Maine Coon is not used to venturing outdoors, it is bound to feel cold most of the time. It is your responsibility to ensure that your cat sleeps in warm beddings in addition to taking it out to receive sunshine when it is possible.

One fact you need to remain alive to when your cat ages is the fact that its immunity reduces, making it highly susceptible to many infections. It becomes very necessary to take your cat to a vet whenever you notice any strange behaviour or symptoms for immediate vet care.

Although Maine Coons are people-oriented pets, your aging Maine Coon cat will be more attention-seeking than at any other time. This is because it naturally knows that it is incapacitated in many ways and will want to be near you most of the time for comfort, assurance and help. Your cat will however tend to sleep for much longer time.

Because of the many behavioural and physiological changes that your cat is bound to go through once the aging process sets in, it

Chapter 13 - Caring for Your Aging Maine Coon

is most likely to engage less in physical activities. It is however very important that you exercise your cat's mind. Limited physical exercise is also necessary to help your cat overcome any discomfort it may experience because of such diseases as arthritis, which aging cats are highly susceptible to.

Health Challenges in Old Cats

Your aging Maine Coon cat experiences a lot of changes including reduced immunity. This exposes it to many diseases/health conditions that you must take note of with the aim of helping it cope. Some of the health challenges your cat is most likely to face include:

Parasite Infestation

Your aging Maine Coon will probably not groom itself as it used to do. This exposes it to parasite infestation and in particular ticks and fleas. This will likely happen if it is used to going outdoors. Infestation of these parasites will easily lead to skin infections. The likelihood of your cat becoming anaemic also becomes high. This is when it becomes necessary to use flea spray or powder. Although you have the alternative of using flea collars, they have the disadvantage of being ineffective. Furthermore, flea collars can also cause allergic reaction. Your cat is also likely to have internal parasites in case it is used to going outdoors, just in the same way it used to do when it was a kitten. It becomes necessary for your aging cat to receive treatment for worms and in particular roundworms after every three months.

Blindness

In addition to such health challenges as hearing loss and loss of memory, a major challenge that your aging Maine Coon is likely to face is blindness. This starts as partial loss of vision before developing into total blindness.

Although you may not be able to know when your cat is loosing its vision, there are specific signs you need to look out for. These include reluctance to move, misjudging heights, clumsiness, eye

Chapter 13 - Caring for Your Aging Maine Coon

rubbing, large pupils and when it easily gets startled. Because treating blindness due to old age is simply impossible, the best you can do to help your cat cope is ensure that it moves in a secure environment, offer help all the time and speaking to it often.

Pain
Such diseases/health conditions as arthritis that your aging Maine Coon is susceptible to are usually accompanied with pain. Your cat may tremble, shiver or crouch. It becomes very important to understand your cat's body language with the aim of offering help. It becomes necessary to take your cat to a vet for proper diagnosis of existing disease and for appropriate pain medications.

Dental Infections
Old cats are highly susceptible to dental infections. Indeed about 70% of all old cats suffer from dental infections mostly caused by formation of plaque. It is during your cat's old age that you must ensure that it receives regular dental care that involves removal of plaque that forms tartar, which in effect leads to gingivitis.

Arthritis
Arthritis is the most common health problem that cats in old age suffer from, just like in humans. This health condition is usually accompanied by joint pain, pain that can make your cat very uncomfortable. Your cat will find it very difficult to engage in physical activities. The best way to help your cat cope is to consult with a local vet for the best supplements to buy; supplements that support the rebuilding of joint cartilage.

Reduced Heart Function
Just like in humans, your cat's heart function reduces once old age sets in. Its heart muscles do not only weaken but also enlarge. It becomes necessary to take your cat to a vet for regular check ups and medications that strengthen heart muscles.

Chapter 14 - What to Do with and Old Maine Coon

Chapter 14 – What to Do with an Old Maine Coon

Living with an old cat or an old Maine Coon cat for that matter can be a serious challenge, especially if it becomes senile. You simply will not cope with the amount of care it needs to continue living comfortably. It is because of this that you may look for alternative ways on how your cat can still receive proper care until when it dies. You have three options:

Cat Rescue Centre

Taking your aged Maine Coon cat to a dedicated cat rescue centre may be your only option of letting your aged cat go. Although it can be very difficult, doing so will lessen your burden of having to watch over it all the time.

Cat rescue centres are institutions established by such organizations as animal welfare societies. Such centres are usually staffed with qualified pet personnel with the necessary skills on taking care of pets of all ages. In addition to admitting aged pets including cats at a small fee, they also offer younger pets for adoption. Such do include rescued pets or those born in such institutions.

Most cat rescue centres are funded by donations received from pet lovers and other organizations. Some well established cat rescue centres serve as educational institutions where pet lovers have the opportunity to learn more about pets they are interested in buying or adopting.

Taking your old Maine Coon to a cat rescue centre does not in any way mean disposing it off. Most rescue centres allow owners

Chapter 14 - What to Do with and Old Maine Coon

to visit their aged cats, a good opportunity to reconnect with pets they have lived with for a long time.

Euthanasia

Euthanasia is the other route or option you have when it comes to dealing with your old cat. Most cat owners whose cats are aged choose to have their cats euthanized instead of taking them to cat rescue centres. The main reason for this is the fact that having their cats euthanized eliminates the worry they would otherwise continuously have over their pets at such centres.

Simply put, euthanasia is the practice where life is ended. You may choose to have your aged cat euthanized in order to relieve it from the pain, anguish, suffering and discomfort it goes through as it waits for its natural death. Different jurisdictions have different laws relating to euthanasia for humans and pets. Your vet should be in a good position to enlighten you on what laws apply in your jurisdiction.

Just like in the case of humans, a vet will normally require that you sign a consent form before euthanizing your cat. The signing of the form absolves a vet from any claim you make thereafter that he/she caused your cat's death. There are however certain instances where vets request pet owners for permission to euthanize their aged pets. Such cases are usually when vets discover serious diseases in the cause of treating cats. Even in such situations, cat owners have the last word on whether or not their cats should be euthanized.

Whether you take your cat to a vet clinic to be euthanized or call a vet to undertake the procedure at home, the procedure is the same. The procedure normally involves giving an over-dose of anaesthesia into the main vein in one of its forelegs. In case of difficult or troublesome cats, a crush cage is normally used.

Injection of anaesthesia leads to immediate unconsciousness followed by slow death. Your cat is most likely to exhale and pass

Chapter 14 - What to Do with and Old Maine Coon

urine as body muscles relax after death. To ensure that your cat is indeed dead, a vet may give additional injection of anaesthesia into the kidney or the heart. Your lovely cat will most likely die with eyes open and a vet will simply close the eyes before placing the cat in a position where it appears to be just asleep. It is only after this that a vet wraps your cat in a black bag both for safety and privacy before handing the same over to you.

Watching your cat die can be a very traumatizing experience. The experience can remain in your mind for a very long time. This is why some cat owners choose to remain in a separate room when a vet undertakes euthanasia on their aged cats and other pets.

Most cat owners do choose to call a vet to perform the procedure in their homes rather than at a vet's clinic, a move that you too may consider.

This is because having the procedure undertaken at home is somehow less traumatic.

The cost of euthanasia varies from one region to another and from one vet to another. The cost can actually be on the higher side if you choose to call a vet to undertake the procedure at home. Generally, the cost ranges between $30 and $80 (£17- £35) across the world. It is always recommended that you settle any outstanding amount with a vet before he/she undertakes the procedure. This is because you may not find it comfortable talking about payments when your cat is already dead.

Home Care
You may choose not to take your aged Maine Coon to a cat rescue centre or have it euthanized. You may take this route if you are fond of your cat and have the time to provide it with all the necessary care it needs until it dies natural death. Although most cat owners choose to care for their cats at home until they die, the suffering, pain and anguish they go through can similarly be traumatizing.

Chapter 14 - What to Do with and Old Maine Coon

Taking your aged cat to a cat rescue centre may eliminate your responsibility to dispose off the body when it finally dies. This will depend on the agreement between you and a care centre management. Most centres do undertake to dispose off bodies of dead cats. Depending on your arrangement, you may be informed. Having your cat euthanized at a vet's clinic, at home or if you choose to care for your cat at home, you will have to determine how to dispose off the body.

Body Disposal

Burial of pets is fast becoming popular around the world and it is highly possible that you too may choose to bury your Maine Coon cat when it finally dies. Even so, you need to acquaint yourself with your local by-laws that relate to disposal of dead pet bodies. You will need to bury your cat soon enough before it putrefies unless you have a freezer where you can store the body for a few days. You may choose to bury your cat in your back garden or at your local authority's pet cemetery.

Even so, there are instances when you may not be allowed to bury your cat. Such are instances where the body poses a degree of risk to human health. This may apply if your cat dies of rabies in which case it will be the responsibility of a vet to dispose off the body.

Cremation

Like with burial, cremation is another popular way of disposing off dead bodies. You may choose to have the body of your cat's body cremated to give you the opportunity to bring its ashes home in a jar to scatter in its room/space or simply keep. It is common to find pet cemeteries having pet cremation facilities where you can have your cat cremated.

Taxidermy

You may choose to have your Maine Coon cat taxidermized to at least allow you have it at home although in a static state.

Chapter 14 - What to Do with and Old Maine Coon

Taxidermy is a process where a professional taxidermist removes all the cat's internal organs including tissue and bones. The remaining skin is then stuffed to make your dead cat look real.

Desiccation

At times referred to as freeze-drying, desiccation is the process where water is removed from your cat's body. Your cat will simply be put in the right posture before being desiccated. The process can take as long as six months and most cat owners do like the result because of its lifelike nature. Because of environmental factors, the desiccated body is usually housed in a glass container for preservation. This gives you the opportunity to have your cat at home even though dead.

Resin Preservation

This is another way you may choose to dispose of your dead Maine Coon's body. It involves removal of blood and other body fluids, which are replaced with resin. Resin has the characteristic of setting in solid, which in effect yields a lifelike body.

Post-Disposal Period

The period soon after disposing of your cat's body can be a very trying time. It can indeed be a trying time in case you have another Maine Coon cat and other pets at home. Do cats have feelings? Will they realize that one of them is missing? How will they cope knowing that one of them is missing? It is a fact that cats have feelings. Maine Coons in particular develop a strong bond between them and will therefore be troubled with absence of one of their own.

One thing you may notice when you have two Maine Coons as pets is that each of them marks its own territory. One of them naturally becomes the leader of the other. The absence of one of them therefore traumatizes the remaining one. It may take some time before the remaining one adjusts. The best way to comfort the remaining one is to always give it as much attention as possible.

Chapter 14 - What to Do with and Old Maine Coon

The situation can be very complicated to handle in case you have children. This is because Maine Coons get a long very well with children because of their playful nature. Your dead cat will not have just been your kids' companion but a valuable playmate. They are bound to take its death very hard. The best you can do in such a situation is to make your kids understand what death is and why their playmate has died.

Making your kids understand what death is and that it applies to human being can be very beneficial to them. This is because kids learn through experiences and knowing about death will make them appreciate the fact that death is natural and can happen to any family member at any time.

How to Cope with Your Maine Coon Cat's Death

Your cat's death can be similar to death of your child or a young family member. Knowing that you adopted or bought it, natured it to maturity and was a valuable companion that is no more can take a toll on your mind. Not only will you develop a feeling of loss but will grieve for your cat. You will probably go into state of denial, develop anger and mourn before accepting that your lovely Maine Coon is no more. This may be the appropriate time to share your feelings with other family members. Doing so will no doubt go a long way in overcoming your anger and feeling of loss you may develop.

One reason why many cat owners choose to dispose of bodies of their cats is to have the opportunity to remember their cats knowing that it is buried in their backyards. Remembrance provides you and your family with a good opportunity to reflect back on the good times you had with your dead cat.

Replacing Your Dead Maine Coon Cat

Having lived with a Maine Coon cat that is no more will most likely drive you to adopt or buy another to replace the dead one.

Chapter 14 - What to Do with and Old Maine Coon

When to have another one will however depend on several factors. One of the most important factors that may make it necessary to have another Maine Coon soon after the death of the previous one is if you had two of them.

The loneliness that the remaining one will feel may make it necessary to get another one for company. You may also need to have another one soon after in case you have children. The other reason why you may need to replace your dead cat soon relates to why you bought or adopted the dead one in the first place. You may simply like pets and Maine Coons in particular. You may also be used to having a pet as a companion and cannot do without one.

Chapter 15 – Becoming a Maine Coon Cat Breeder

Who is a Breeder?
With its beautiful long fur, dominating figure, perfect disposition, high intelligence and its playful nature, you may choose to become a Maine Coon cat breeder. The Maine Coon breed is indeed a very popular breed in the world and becoming a breeder of the same can assure you of a ready market, depending on your location.

Basically, a breeder is one who is engaged in the business of mating carefully selected animals or plants to reproduce offspring that exhibit specific qualities and characteristics unique to a breed. Becoming a Maine Coon cat breeder therefore involves breeding pure-bred Maine Coons with the aim of reproducing kittens that exhibit qualities and characteristics unique to the breed.

You can become a breeder purely for fun as a hobby or as a business. Whether you choose to breed as a hobby or as a business, you will have a good opportunity to participate in professional cat shows and competitions. Becoming a breeder does not require that you must have attained a specific level of education. You must however demonstrate that you have compassion and a genuine interest in the Maine Coon breed.

Things to Note
Although you may have compassion and interest in the Maine Coon breed to a point where you want to become a breeder of the same, there are important things you need to take note of. From the onset, becoming a Maine Coon breeder will not make you rich

Chapter 15 - Becoming a Maine Coon Cat Breeder

overnight. Becoming a breeder can be very expensive and you should not expect to recoup your expenses within a short period. You need to start breeding as a hobby before you can expect to start receiving some income. Indeed, most current successful Maine Coon breeders started off breeding as a hobby before graduating to full time commercial breeders.

The second thing to note is that the practice of breeding requires commitment, devotion and time. Time in particular is very important. It becomes very necessary that you devote most of your time to your cattery. This is because the cattery requires daily cleaning, feeding, grooming and treatment of your cats. This is the only way you will be able to breed healthy Maine Coons that will encourage many in your neighbourhood to buy.

Third, becoming a breeder requires some level of financial investment. You will need to construct a cattery at a suitable location, install the necessary infrastructure, buy cat food and engage the service of a vet among other costs. You will also need to incur other expenses in having your cats registered by relevant bodies and pay some fee to your local authority. Most current Maine Coon breeders stated off with only two cats in small rooms right within their homes, something that you too may consider.

Lastly, you need to be prepared to handle emotional toll that comes along with the practice of breeding. The fact that you will be taking care of many cats and mating them means that they will be giving birth. It is common for some pregnant cats to die when giving birth in catteries. Others will die of natural causes including diseases. Kittens will also be at risk of dying of natural causes. Watching as your lovely Maine Coons and kittens die will take a serious toll on your mind.

Chapter 15 - Becoming a Maine Coon Cat Breeder

General Breeding Information

The best way to start off as a breeder is to prepare a room in your homestead to serve as your cattery on a temporary basis. This is not only cost effective; it will also be easy to manage your cats. Such preparation involves equipping the room with all the necessary equipment and supplies your cats will need to survive. These include food, water/food dishes, scratch post, bed and beddings and cat play toys among other equipment and supplies. You also need to engage the service of a veterinarian who will be responsible for treating your cats whenever they fall sick, get injured and in giving vaccinations.

The second step to becoming a Maine Coon cat breeder is identifying an established breeder to buy kittens or cats from. It is mandatory that you buy from an established and registered breeder. This is because such a breeder will be breeding pedigree properly registered Maine Coon cats.

You have the option of buying a female cat (queens), in which case you will be obligated to buy a male (tom) afterwards or take the queen to a vet or breeder for insemination. You also have the option of buying two Maine Coons; a tom and a queen. Depending on your preference and level of preparedness in becoming a breeder, you may choose to buy kittens or adult cats.

The fourth step to becoming a breeder is to register as a breeder. You have several options on how to register, depending on your location and preference. There are both national and international cat registries from which you can choose one to register with. International cat registries include UK's Cat Fanciers Association (CFA), France's Federation Internationale Feline (FIFe), UAE's Emirates Feline Federation (EFF), The American Cat Fanciers Association (ACFA) and The International Cat Association (TICA). National cat registries include UK's Governing Council of the Cat Fancy (GCCF), UK's Felis Britannica (member of

Chapter 15 - Becoming a Maine Coon Cat Breeder

FIFe), PRC's Cat Aficionado Association (CAA) and the Canadian Cat Association (CCA) among other national registries.

Registering your cats provides for several benefits. First, you will be recognized as a registered breeder licensed to breed Maine Coons. Secondly, you will have the opportunity to participate in both national and international cat shows and have your cats participate in different championships depending on their age. Participation in such championships can earn you good money depending on how your cats perform.

Thirdly, you will have the opportunity to learn better breeding techniques both from a registry you register with and other Maine Coon cat breeders. Registering as a breeder also gives you the opportunity to know the exact breed standards you will have to maintain as a Maine Coon cat breeder. Lastly, you will have the opportunity to be appointed as a Maine Coon show judge after gaining reasonable breeding experience and if you so wish. Note that you can register with more than one registry if you so wish so long as you are financially capable of meeting all registration fees.

Different cat registries do organize different Maine Coon cat shows and competitions. CFA for example organizes the Kitten Shows and Championships (for pedigreed kittens aged between one and three years), Championships (for unaltered cats aged eight months), Premiership (for altered cats aged above two year), Veteran (for both altered and unaltered cats aged seven years) and Household (for non-pedigreed cats aged two years months).

Successful registration as a Maine Coon cat breeder is just the first step to becoming a professional breeder. Because the cats you buy will have been registered by their breeder, you will need to register the litter that your cats give birth to. This you will do with a registry you registered with. Registering your litter entitles you to a unique prefix that will hence forth be used as the first

Chapter 15 - Becoming a Maine Coon Cat Breeder

name for all litter that your cats will produce. It will be your responsibility to indicate a prefix you will wish to use.

Different cat registries have different requirements when registering prefixes. The GCCF for example requires that you must have been registered as a breeder for at least one year before you can register your litter.

Unlike most cat breeds, Maine Coons do not become sexually active until they attain an average age of two years. Both your tom and queen become sexually active with the queen capable of attaining pregnancy when it is between two and three years. You will be able to know when your queen is on heat when it becomes too vocal and lies on the floor as if presenting itself to a male. Your queen's gestation period is between 60 and 65 days. The last week of pregnancy will see your queen look for the most appropriate place to give birth. It will look for dark yet safe place where to give forth its litter. Maine Coons generally give birth to very few litters, between two and three litters on average.

Building a Cattery

It is only appropriate that you build a cattery once you have established yourself as a Maine Coon cat breeder. A cattery is where you house your cats for commercial purpose. Although yours will be a breeding cattery, you will also have the option of using it as a boarding cattery in which case other cat owners not able to travel with their cats will bring their cats to you for safe keeping at a fee.

It is mandatory that you apply for a license from your local authority before you can build a cattery. You also need to follow cattery building guidelines provided by a registry you register with. Every registry has minimum cattery construction requirements that you must stick to before you can receive another license from the registrar. A registrar will only grant you a cattery license after inspecting your cattery and certifying it to

Chapter 15 - Becoming a Maine Coon Cat Breeder

have met the set minimum construction requirements. Most registrars engage the service of local veterinarians to undertake search inspections. It will be the responsibility of the appointed vet to inspect your cattery on a regular basis to ensure that you stick to set breeding guidelines.

There are several minimum requirements when it comes to constructing a cattery one of which is space. You cattery needs to be spacious enough to accommodate all your cats comfortably. The minimum space per cat is set at 30 cubic feet. In addition, you need to create a space for play, grooming and maintenance. Established breeders do go the extra mile to group and house their stock according to their age, groups that are housed in separated cages as one way of preventing diseases. The other very important minimum requirement you need to meet is to construct your cattery in such a way that it allows for free flow of fresh air for your cats' good health. Your cattery should not only have enough windows but large enough windows that allow for free flow or air in and out of the cattery. The fact that Maine Coons are both indoor and outdoor pets makes it very necessary that you have windows that allow sufficient amount of light into the cattery. Artificial lighting may be necessary to achieve this if the windows do not provide for sufficient natural light.

Cat registrars are very strict when it comes to cattery sanitation. Not only are you required to construct your cattery in a clean environment; you will also need to ensure that there is high standard of cleanliness in and around your cattery on a daily basis. Sanitation is one of the most important things that an appointed veterinarian will always pay attention to whenever he/she pays a visit to your cattery.

Such guidelines are not only requirements, they are mandatory taking into account the fact that failure to observe the same can lead to occurrence of cat diseases that can wipe out your cat population. Apart from such guidelines, you will need to have all

Chapter 15 - Becoming a Maine Coon Cat Breeder

the necessary supplies and equipment that your cats will need for good health and play activities. You will also need to engage the service of a veterinarian who will be available whenever situation demand and when it is time for vaccinations.

Chapter 16 – International & National Cat Organizations, Associations and Clubs

There are many international and national organizations, associations and clubs that are in the business of promoting and maintaining welfare of specific cat breeds including the Maine Coon breed. Most of the international and national organizations and associations are indeed cat registries. Cat clubs in particular are of special mention because they limit themselves to specific cat breeds including the Maine Coon cat breed. Most clubs happen to be established by cat owners. Below are just a few of the notable organizations, associations and clubs.

The American Cat Fanciers Association (ACFA)

Founded in 1955, ACFA serves the interest of cat breeders, cat owners, exhibitors and the general public in different ways. The association largely engages in promoting welfare, providing education, knowledge and enhancing interest of domesticated cats, both purebred and non-purebred.

Membership to ACFA is open to all including members of the public with interest in cats. Members receive several benefits including a copy of the association's regularly published ACFA bulletin that is published seven times in a year. Members also have access to many cat articles on the association's website, articles written by professional cat breeders and vets.

Membership to ACFA also entitles one to vote in the association's yearly elections. Members have the obligation to

Chapter 16 - International and National Cat Organizations, Associations and Clubs

elect from among themselves who to represent them in the association's board of directors. ACFA is also a cat registry that you can register your litters with as a breeder at massive discount.

ACFA organizes cat shows at different locations in the USA, an activity that gives cat owners an opportunity to show-case their pets and possibly win show awards.

The Cat Fanciers' Association (CFA)

Founded in 1906 in the USA, CFA is the world's largest cat registry of pedigree cats. Headquartered in Ohio, the association has a mission to preserve and promote pedigree breeds of cats with the aim of enhancing their well-being. CFA current cat breed registration stands at 43 including the Maine Coon cat breed. CFA has witnessed unprecedented growth since 2006 after its centennial celebrations, growth that has seen the association recognize 39 breeds for its Championship Class.
In addition to registering cat breeds, CFA also offers several other services to purebred cat owners, catteries and the general public. It indeed has registered cat pedigrees that date three generations back.

Perhaps one of the most memorable moments for CFA was in 1994 when it hosted the CFA International Cat Show, the largest in USA cat shows. In addition to organizing cat shows, CFA is also engaged in setting and enforcing cat breed standards through cattery inspections, training cat show judges, supporting and publicizing research on cat issues, influencing cat legislation agendas and running cat breed rescue programs.

Cat Owners Association of Western Australia (COAWA)

Founded in 1992 in Western Australia, COAWA exists as a cat registry and an advisory body to the Coordinating Cat Council of

Chapter 16 - International and National Cat Organizations, Associations and Clubs

Australia. COAWA registers pedigree cats and provides a platform where cat breeders, cat owners and members of the public meet. It also registers non-pedigree cats.

In addition to cat breed registration, COAWA also organizes cat shows including kitten and adult championship shows. The association currently has four cat clubs affiliated to it and boasts of a good number of cat breed judges.

The Governing Council of the Cat Fancy (GCCF)

Founded in 1910, GCCF is the largest cat registry in the UK. It largely registers pedigree cats. GCCF was founded by smaller cat registries and is now an independent council with over 150 member clubs including Maine Coon cat clubs across the UK. In addition to being a cat registry, GCCF also licenses cat shows organized by all cat clubs affiliated to it. It currently licenses over 100 cat shows every year. Apart from licensing cat shows organized by its clubs, GCCF also organizes its own cat show dubbed the Supreme Cat Show, which is usually the largest cat show in the world.

The International Cat Association (TICA)

TICA is the world's largest single cat association. Its membership comprises of catteries, cat owners and people interested in cats. Based in the USA, TICA draws its membership from across the globe including from Africa, Latin America, North America, Europe and Asia. It is a cat genetic registry that also registers new cat breeds. In addition to registering pedigree cat breeds, TICA also registers non-pedigree household cats that enjoy the same status as pedigree cats in terms of cat shows and awards.

In an effort to enhance cat breeding, TICA has an elaborate Junior Exhibition specially tailored for children who love cats, giving

Chapter 16 - *International and National Cat Organizations, Associations and Clubs*

them a good opportunity to graduate to senior levels as cat breeders.

TICA has clear responsibilities that include registration of both pedigree and non-pedigree litters, formulation of regulations for management of cat associations, licensing of cat shows organized by its members, establishing cat breed standards, dissemination of cat breed information, organization of cat exhibitions and education of cat owners among other responsibilities.

World Pet Association (WPA)

WPA is a body that exists to bring pet food manufacturers and pet owners together. It allows for the two parties to interact through education and sharing of information. Most of its members happen to be cat food manufacturers, cat breeders, cat organizations and associations. WPA is basically the cat industry's premier trade association. It plays a very important role in disseminating information, educating and supporting research related to cat food.

World Cat Congress (WCC)

WCC is a confederation of the largest international and national cat organizations and associations. It exists to promote understanding and cooperation among all the organizations and associations on matters that concern them. It encourages international cooperation among its membership on such matters as veterinary issues, legislations, pedigree issues and other related matters. Its membership includes FIFe, CFA, TICA, WCF, ACF, GCCF and NZCF among many other international and national organizations/associations.

Chapter 16 - International and National Cat Organizations, Associations and Clubs

United Maine Coon Cat Association (UMCCA)

UMCCA was established in late 1972. It is an association started by CFF's Maine Coon Breed Club. The association was specifically established to protect and promote the Maine Coon cat breed. It is through the association that CFF specified the recommended Maine Coon standard recognized by CFF.

The association draws its membership from US, England and Australia. Although most of its members happen to be Maine Coon cat breeders, individual Maine Coon owners are also accepted as members.

Maine Coon Cat Club

This club has its base in the UK and was established in 1985. It was established by the first Maine Coon cat owners who introduced the breed in the UK in 1984. Establishment of the club effectively replaced the British Maine Coon Cat Club with the aim of becoming a GCCF affiliate.

In addition to organizing its own Maine Coon cat championship shows, the club also hosts various social functions and seminars aimed at promoting the Maine Coon cat breed.

Maine Coon Breed Society

Maine Coon Cat Club is based in the UK and is affiliated to GCCF. The society aims at maintaining Maine Coon cat standard in the UK for the benefit of Maine Coon cat owners and lovers in the UK. Membership to the society is open to both Maine Coon cat breeders and owners alike.

Joining any of these organizations/associations, societies or clubs provides for several benefits particularly in case you wish to be a

Chapter 16 - International and National Cat Organizations, Associations and Clubs

Maine Coon Catt breeder. Such benefits include breed information, breed standards and general breeding information. You also get the opportunity to take part in many international and national cat shows and championships organized in different regions across the world throughout any given year. Joining any of the organizations also gives you a good opportunity to become a cat judge at cat shows and championships, the ultimate dream of many cat breeders and dedicated cat owners.

Conclusion

Cats and Maine Coon cats in particular make very good pets. Not only is the Maine Coon attractive; it is adorable as well. You will never feel bored when living with a Maine Coon. It is a playful cat that engages you all the time. It will always want you to give it attention, which is perfectly normal since it may be the only trusted companion you can have at home.

The Maine Coon is one cat that does not discriminate when it comes to family members. It is particularly very good with children to who it develops a very strong bond because of its playful nature. Furthermore, the cat is very receptive to training.

According to research studies published in the Journal of Vascular and Interventional Neurology, living with a cat provides for several health benefits. One of the main benefits is that living with a cat reduces the risk of suffering from cardiovascular diseases including heart attack. Other health benefits associated with living with a cat include reduced risk of high stress level, reduced cholesterol level and reduced risk of depression.

Children raised in an environment where there is a cat have also been noted to grow up healthier than those raised in an environment where there is none. Unlike most cat breeds, the Maine Coon breed is very cost effective so long as you give it proper care. It is generally a healthy breed that is less susceptible to common diseases that other cat breeds are highly susceptible to. The fact that the breed's kittens do not inherit serious diseases/health conditions translates into reduced veterinary expenses.

Conclusion

The popularity of the Maine Coon across the globe is not in doubt. It is one of the top cat breeds that most home owners prefer to have in their homes as indoor and outdoor pets. Its' popularity is also evident in the increasing number of cat breeders registering with different cat registries around the world. It is also not surprising that dedicated Maine Coon cat clubs are also being established in different regions around the world.

You can choose to have two Maine Coons as indoor and outdoor pets or join the big league as a Maine Coon breeder. While you will have a loyal, lovely, obedient and a valuable companion if you choose to have them as pets, you are also most likely to excel as a breeder should you decide to go that route.

Published by IMB Publishing 2014

Copyright and Trademarks. This publication is Copyright 2014 by IMB Publishing. All products, publications, software and services mentioned and recommended in this publication are protected by trademarks. In such instance, all trademarks & copyright belong to the respective owners. All rights reserved. No part of this book may be reproduced or transferred in any form or by any means, graphic, electronic, or mechanical, including photocopying, recording, taping, or by any information storage retrieval system, without the written permission of the author. Pictures used in this book are either royalty free pictures bought from stock-photo websites or have the source mentioned underneath the picture. Disclaimer and Legal Notice. This product is not legal or medical advice and should not be interpreted in that manner. You need to do your own due-diligence to determine if the content of this product is right for you. The author and the affiliates of this product are not liable for any damages or losses associated with the content in this product. While every attempt has been made to verify the information shared in this publication, neither the author nor the affiliates assume any responsibility for errors, omissions or contrary interpretation of the subject matter herein. Any perceived slights to any specific person(s) or organization(s) are purely unintentional. We have no control over the nature, content and availability of the web sites listed in this book. The inclusion of any web site links does not necessarily imply a recommendation or endorse the views expressed within them. IMB Publishing takes no responsibility for, and will not be liable for, the websites being temporarily unavailable or being removed from the internet. The accuracy and completeness of information provided herein and opinions stated herein are not guaranteed or warranted to produce any particular results, and the advice and strategies, contained herein may not be suitable for every individual. The author shall not be liable for any loss incurred as a consequence of the use and application, directly or indirectly, of any information presented in this work. This publication is designed to provide information in regards to the subject matter covered. The information included in this book has been compiled to give an overview of the subject s and detail some of the symptoms, treatments etc. that are available to people with this condition. It is not intended to give medical advice. For a firm diagnosis of your condition, and for a treatment plan suitable for you, you should consult your doctor or consultant. The writer of this book and the publisher are not responsible for any damages or negative consequences following any of the treatments or methods highlighted in this book. Website links are for informational purposes and should not be seen as a personal endorsement; the same applies to the products detailed in this book. The reader should also be aware that although the web links included were correct at the time of writing, they may become out of date in the future.

CPSIA information can be obtained
at www.ICGtesting.com
Printed in the USA
BVHW080936151020
591023BV00011B/867